Praise for *Staying in the Game*

"Twenty years ago we looked at emotional intelligence as the leadership differentiator. Today, it's agility. Pamela Meyer is to agility what Daniel Goleman is to emotional intelligence. *Staying in the Game* is the guide every leader needs to grow, learn, lead, and thrive in today's dynamic environment."

Melissa Davis, VP Talent Management at Seagen

"*Staying in the Game* is an extraordinary testament to the power of resilience, adaptability, and the indomitable human spirit. It is a must-read for anyone who wants to continue to thrive and make an impact, whether on the slopes or in the boardroom."

Bill Madsen, Director of NASTAR at Outside,
Mayor of Snowmass Village, Colorado

"*Staying in the Game* offers a welcome fresh perspective that invites leaders at all levels of the organization to practice Embodied Agile Leadership. In addition to preparing leaders to be effective in dynamic conditions, they will discover how to nurture an environment of innovation and collaboration where top talent can thrive."

Angela E.L. Barnes, Chief Legal Officer at IDEO

"This thought-provoking and engaging read is filled with vivid stories that had my brain reeling with ideas for my everyday life and work. I thoroughly enjoyed how the book deepened my understanding of "the game" and gave me fresh insights for leading and learning with agility."

Jessie Heath, Director of Global Talent, Culture & Inclusion at La-Z-Boy, Incorporated

"I am so excited for others to pick up this book because they will also not want to put it down! The inspiring, diverse, and relatable stories and reflective questions serve as a leadership manual for anyone wanting to up their game in their current role or prepare for their next one."

J'ai Brown, VP, Human Resources at Hub International

"Pamela's got game! And you can have it, too. In her new must-read book, she shows us how to lead and effect positive change and make real whatever it is we seek."

David Grossman, Leadership and communications expert and author of *Heart First: Lasting Leader Lessons from a Year That Changed Everything*

"*Staying in the Game* is a revelation for the future of work and leadership. Any leader who wants to be successful in today's ever-changing environment must have a growth mindset that builds the muscle of in-the-moment reflection to lead intentionally and authentically. Through inspiring examples on varied terrain, readers learn how to apply the principles of Embodied Agile Leadership and sharpen their purpose and impact."

Jeanette Johnson, Chief People Officer at Surepoint Technologies

"What a joyful read! *Staying in the Game* reminded me of the many lessons I have learned leading a fast-paced, growing company. Rather than bracing for the unexpected, each chapter inspires readers to embrace challenging moments at the peak of the game. Instead of wishing them away, you will learn to embrace these moments as opportunities to become better for the next game that awaits you. Thank you, Pamela Meyer, for reminding us that we don't need to have all of the answers but rather showing us how to develop the confidence to navigate each situation to a positive outcome by being fully engaged, staying agile, and leading with our whole selves."

Erik S. Dodier, Co-founder & CEO at RafterOne

"*Staying in the Game* is a brilliant road map for what's next. Pamela Meyer beautifully describes how people and organizations can succeed personally and professionally while purposefully empowering teams. The dynamic future requires all of us to be agile and 'get comfortable being uncomfortable.' Pamela lights the way through easily consumed nuggets and inspiring examples that make the process seem natural and achievable, even for a novice. After reading this book, I feel like I just engaged a shrink for my corporate self and I have a positive picture of what the future can be!"

Paul Salasky, Senior Business Development Manager at Experis

Staying in the Game

Leading and Learning with **AGILITY** for a Dynamic Future

PAMELA MEYER

RISE LINE

Staying in the Game: Leading and Learning with Agility for a Dynamic Future
© 2023 Pamela Meyer

Published by Rise Line Media.

All rights reserved. No part of this book may be reproduced or used in any manner without the prior written permission of the copyright owner, except for the use of brief quotations in a book review or as permitted by US copyright law.

To request permissions, contact the author.

Printed in the United States of America.
First paperback edition August 2023.

Cover and layout design by G Sharp Design, LLC.
www.gsharpmajor.com

ISBN 979-8-9887094-0-4 (paperback)
ISBN 979-8-9887094-1-1 (hardcover)

To all the embodied agile leaders on and off the mountain who continue to inspire me and countless others to stay in the game.

More Books by Pamela Meyer

The Agility Shift:
Creating Agile and Effective Leaders, Teams and Organizations

Permission:
A Guide to Generating More Ideas, Being More of
Yourself and Having More Fun at Work

From Workplace to Playspace:
Innovating, Learning and Changing Through Dynamic Engagement

Quantum Creativity:
Nine Principles to Transform the Way You Work

TABLE OF CONTENTS

Foreword xv
Introduction 1

PART I 11
THE GAME

Chapter 1	**What Is the Game?** 13
	Discovering Your Four Ps
Chapter 2	**Why Stay in the GAME?** 27
	Leading and Learning with Your Embodied Agile Self
Chapter 3	**What's Stopping YOU?** 39
	Realistically Assessing Risks and Reaping Rewards
Chapter 4	**Leading with Learning** 57
	Transforming Barriers into Growth Opportunities

PART II 77
THE DYNAMICS OF BEING IN THE GAME

Chapter 5	**Meaningful Identity** 79
	Naming and Claiming Your Core
Chapter 6	**Community** 101
	Tapping the Power of People
Chapter 7	**Competition** 125
	Learning for Life
Chapter 8	**Commitment** 145
	Prioritizing, Persevering, and Adapting

PART III 169
STAYING AND PLAYING FOR LIFE AND LIVELIHOOD

Chapter 9	**Staying Agile and Relevant** 171
Chapter 10	**Staying Strong and Resilient** 183
Chapter 11	**Staying Happy** 205
Chapter 12	**A Special Note to the C-Suite** 221
	Leading and Learning with Agility for a Dynamic Future

Acknowledgments 240
About the Author 242
Chapter Notes 244
More Reading and Resources 259
Index 263

FOREWORD

I've always believed in listening to your gut. It has a way of slicing through the clutter, signaling when something is off kilter. However, confronting the uncomfortable truth your gut reveals can be difficult.

Back in the early 2000s, I was working as a Technical Project Manager for a large software company. My job was to drive delivery dates from various functional managers months in advance and enter them into complex Excel spreadsheets. This exercise was supposed to help us achieve our strategic goals on time and on budget. But something felt wrong. My gut was telling me that this approach was flawed. How could we predict the future with such certainty? What if things changed along the way? What if our assumptions were wrong? And most importantly, what if our customers' needs were different from what we thought they were?

As I tried to follow the established "best practices" of project management, I felt a growing tension in my body and mind. I had an MBA and a PMP certification but felt like I was failing. Our projects were often late, over budget, or irrelevant to our customers.

This tension, it turns out, was a sign of a deeper truth. The traditional ways of working were not suitable for dynamic and uncertain environments. They were based on false assumptions and outdated paradigms. They were ignoring the reality of complexity and change.

The realization led me to explore agile methodologies, a shift that brought relief and a renewed sense of purpose to my professional life. I no longer had to ignore what my gut was telling me—agile ways of working just made sense. They were aligned with the principles of complexity science, human psychology, and customer-centricity.

Today, agile is no longer a niche or a novelty. It has become the mainstream and expected way of working in many industries and domains. Business agility is seen as a vital catalyst for growth, innovation, and customer satisfaction. I have been fortunate to lead several large-scale agile transformations and have experienced first-hand the very real impact that working in agile ways has on organizations and their people. Yet, sustaining agile transformations is proving to be a challenge. It is sad to see organizations that have successfully adopted agile ways of thinking gradually slide back to more traditional, plan-driven mindsets.

It turns out that becoming more agile—as hard as it can be—is no match for *remaining* agile. Continuing to improve and adapt every day requires a different kind of leadership, one that is not based on command and control but on empowerment and learning.

In my journey as an agile leader, I've been captivated by the quest to build and maintain agile organizations capable of flourishing amid uncertainty. I have encountered the hurdles and rewards of embracing agility as a mindset, a culture, and a way of working, learning invaluable lessons from fellow agile practitioners and thought leaders worldwide.

This is why I was delighted to read *Staying in the Game* by Pamela Meyer, a book that offers a fresh and compelling perspective on agile leadership for a dynamic future. Drawing from her extensive research and practice in various fields, including alpine ski racing, improvisation, organizational development, and education, Meyer introduces the concept of Embodied Agile Leadership (EAL) as a way of leading and learning with agility for life and livelihood.

EAL is not a formula or a framework but rather a set of principles and practices that enable leaders to engage their whole selves—body, mind, and spirit—in responding effectively to changing situations and creating positive impact. The dynamics of EAL help leaders find their game, stay in it, and play it with energy, enthusiasm, and impact.

Meyer illustrates EAL with rich and diverse stories from amateur alpine ski racers, entrepreneurs, executives, educators, activists, and others who exemplify its principles in action. She also provides practical coaching questions and tools to help readers reflect on their own experiences and apply the lessons learned to their own contexts.

Staying in the Game is not just a book about agile leadership; it is a book that also *invites* agile leadership. It challenges readers to question their assumptions, experiment with new possibilities, learn from feedback, and adapt to changing conditions. It inspires readers to tap into their passion, purpose, playfulness, and pleasure as sources of motivation and resilience.

I highly recommend *Staying in the Game* to anyone who wants to stay agile, relevant, resilient, and happy in rapidly changing, often unpredictable situations. Whether you are leading yourself or others, whether you are working in business or another domain, or whether you are new or experienced in agile ways of working, you will find valuable perspectives and guidance.

Staying in the Game is more than a book; it is an invitation to join a community of Embodied Agile Leaders who are making a difference in the world. I hope you accept this invitation and discover the power and joy of staying in your game. Your gut will thank you!

Jorgen Hesselberg
Co-founder of *Comparative Agility, LLC,* author of *Unlocking Agility*

INTRODUCTION

An avalanche warning is delaying the race's start. My fellow racers and I are waiting at the top of the giant slalom racecourse at Palisades Tahoe. We've all qualified for the National NASTAR[1] Championships (the largest amateur alpine ski racing competition in the world). The hold on the course and a rumor going around in the start area that it is the steepest course ever set for this national competition has only increased my anxiety. And my anxiety is already high because a cold front moved in overnight after days of rain and froze the snow on our course into a sheet of ice. As I wait, I remind myself that I have raced at this level before, raced on ice before, and raced on steep runs before (okay, maybe not this steep, but steepish). I have trained, prepared my equipment, taken my warm-up runs, and inspected the course. I am ready.

This Is Not an Accident

Standing in that start gate on the side of that icy mountain was not by accident. Not for any of us. We didn't mean to be skiing leisurely on a gentle slope or sipping a hot toddy in front of the fire in the lodge. I was standing at the gate because I love everything about this game: the preparation, the unknown, the challenge of the course, and making countless adjustments at high speeds. I was there because ski racing challenges me to develop and sustain my fitness and agility.

Playing this game also helps me succeed in all the other high-stakes situations that my clients and I negotiate each day in life and work.

I Have Questions

When I returned to alpine ski racing after a 25-year hiatus and began training and competing in earnest, I soon noticed the long-time racers, many of whom were still competing at a high level in their 60s, 70s, and even 80s. The more I watched these athletes, the more questions I had. I wondered what kept them coming back, weekend after weekend, season after season, year after year. What motivated them to stay fit in the off-season and to keep learning and striving to improve? What lessons could I learn from others who were staying in *their* games that could help me get in and stay in the ski racing game—and help others I work with who also want to stay agile, relevant, resilient, strong, and happy in their lives and work? Isn't this what we *all* want?

My research began casually. During chairlift conversations or post-race beers at the lodge, I asked questions as we awaited the official results, weekly raffle prizes, and awards. As themes from these conversations started emerging, my curiosity led me to a more intentional inquiry, interviewing amateur alpine ski racers across the country over the next several years ranging in age from mid 20s to late 80s and identifying as male, female, LGBTQ+, and a diverse mix of races and nationalities.

> Ski racing and life and business, across the board, they're all the same. You have to learn how to adjust and to keep going and to have perseverance. You have to be able to take a risk and learn as you go—and be willing to make mistakes and own those.
>
> —**Amanda Keen, business owner and ski racer**

I was particularly interested in learning from amateurs because the very word *amateur* derives from the Latin "amare," meaning "to love," which perfectly encapsulated my question: "What do you love about this game so much that you are motivated to go to extraordinary lengths to stay in it?" I was particularly interested in the game of ski racing, not only because I had a front-row seat but also because it demands a high level of commitment, a higher-than-average degree of risk, and the ability to maintain a significant level of fitness, all without any big external reward beyond a possible inexpensive medal or end-of-season trophy.

This is where my research began but not where it ended. I soon recognized that the emerging themes were relevant and shared by another equally impressive group: agile leaders in business. Perhaps not surprisingly, I discovered that many of the athletes I interviewed also had successful careers, and many had risen to challenging leadership roles in their organizations. I'm not the first to have noticed this pattern. *Fortune* magazine estimates that as many as 95% of Fortune 500 CEOs played sports,[2] with many continuing rigorous training and competition throughout their careers. Whether the leaders I studied developed their fitness for sport, business, or both, they all developed it intentionally and with their whole selves. This discovery led me to probe for the lessons they transferred from the racecourse to the boardroom, courtroom, international project team, ICU, or other high-stakes arenas.

Making a Metaphor Out of a Mountain

Many of the Embodied Agile Leaders, or EALs, I studied had very little, if any, inclination to test their skills on the ski slopes or in any other athletic arena. However, they all understand the importance of staying meaningfully engaged. EALs know how to find their version of "the game" and commit to a range of practices that enable them to stay in it with energy, enthusiasm, and impact.

Probing further, I discovered these highly engaged and agile leaders shared another quality of whole-person self-awareness and intentionality. This insight led me to name a new type of leadership: Embodied Agile Leadership. You will learn more about this in the coming chapters as well as about each of the dynamics these leaders intentionally practice in their lives and work. It is not a new revelation that successful leadership, especially agile leadership, begins with self-awareness and self-leadership. However, the framework for Embodied Agile Leadership spotlights the critical dimension of *embodiment* that is missing in other conceptions.

> Everything I needed to know in business, I learned skiing.
>
> —**Abbie More, Product Group Manager, FrieslandCampina Ingredients**

Unlike many leadership books that act as if we leave our bodies behind or that our value at work exists only from the neck up, this book brings the whole body, mind, and spirit along for the ride. This is not a coincidence. When we bring our whole selves to work and life, we have access to a much greater source of our creative energy and power; we have a *livelihood*.

You Don't Have to Be Extraordinary (I'm Not)

At this point, you might be tempted to think that this book must be about superhuman people who have been blessed with remarkable circumstances of privilege, resources, or even genetics to be successful agile leaders in business and sports. I used to think this, too, until I got my ordinary self out there along with the other amateur athletes. While I was tempted to give in to excuses, I didn't wait until I was in the best shape of my life or to develop expert skills and abilities. I got out there with my limitations of age, available time, and health (and battling the few extra pounds that come from that magic combination of a slowing metabolism and enjoying an occasional glass of wine) but with a desire to get in the game. On the racecourse, I met others who found their way into the game from across socioeconomic strata, races and ethnicities, sexual orientations, political affiliations, and geographic regions. They came in all shapes, sizes, and ability levels. But all shared a passion for being "in it" and a desire to continue learning and improving.

EALs are remarkable and unremarkable at the same time. They are remarkable in the enthusiasm and commitment that gets them off the couch and out of the house on days and times most of their peers are happy staying in their cozy beds. They are unremarkable in that they make up a cross-section of people with whom you work and live every day. Some face greater social, economic, health, or logistical barriers than others, but all have found a way to overcome them to get in and stay in the game.

Who Should Read This Book and Why

I have a confession to make. I wrote this book because I wanted to read it. I wanted answers to the questions I posed at the start of this introduction to help me stay in the game in my life and livelihood. If you share this curiosity and desire, this book is for you.

This curiosity is also aligned with an urgent need in the global population and within organizations. The annual Microsoft Employment Trends report issued at the height of the COVID-19 pandemic found that 43% of employees were somewhat or extremely likely to consider changing jobs in the coming year, with that number jumping to 52% for Gen Z and millennials.[3] Of those who quit their current jobs, a McKinsey study found that 48% moved to different employers in different industries.[4] This trend persists and highlights an urgent need for leaders at all levels of the organization to foster a climate and practices where everyone thrives. These organizations are discovering that the ability to live into a meaningful purpose while learning and adapting for a dynamic future is essential for sustained success and happiness.

> **The ability to live into a meaningful purpose while learning and adapting for a dynamic future is essential for sustained success and happiness.**

This book is for anyone who wants to stay agile, relevant, resilient, and happy in rapidly changing, often unpredictable situations and for those who want to create environments that support this experience for others in their organizations and wider communities. This type of leadership does not depend on your job title, place in the org chart, or compensation package. It depends on your desire to continue to learn, adapt, and grow.

How to Read This Book

As you read the stories and the lessons learned from the EALs in this book, I encourage you to think about your most engaging and challenging experiences and endeavors. Grounded in your passion, you can build a bridge between the stories and examples of other EALs and your own.

The examples and stories I draw from are varied by design. It is often easier to discern lessons and insight from people who have grappled with challenges in very different settings. As you read, look for the common humanistic denominator that links these experiences to your endeavors. Your experiences very likely demand similar levels of commitment and continuous learning and result in important rewards. My goal is to share compelling insights while allowing you to discover your guiding lessons within the stories. This is how insight transforms into action—and it's more fun, too.

Overview

Staying in the Game is divided into three parts. In Part I, you will discover the What? and Why? of the game, as well as how to assess and overcome obstacles that may be getting in your way. I will also introduce the *Embodied Reflection and Action Framework* that will help you make the most of the lessons you are learning in the book.

Part II focuses on *being* in the game. Through more examples and research, you will deepen your understanding of Embodied Agile Leadership and discover the four dynamics that contribute to EALs' ability to learn, adapt, and innovate at the highest level in their chosen field of play: Meaningful Identity, Community, Competition, and Commitment.

Part III is dedicated to *staying* in the game. Here, I revisit some of the earlier themes, as well as share additional stories, insights, and practices that will enable you to stay agile and relevant, strong and resilient, and happy as you continue engaging in and co-creating your game for a dynamic future.

Coaching

Each chapter of this book concludes with coaching questions for reflection and self-assessment. Many EALs credit the coaching they have received for their ability to stay in the game as they encounter the inevitable setbacks, challenges, obstacles, and opportunities that happen along the way. You can think of these end-of-chapter coaching segments as brief conversations with a personal guide. You will gain personal insight and clarity for effective action through a series of questions. As a leader, you will also gain the confidence to coach yourself and others who wish to get in and stay in the game. I encourage you to keep each chapter's Embodied Reflection and Action Framework handy as you read so that you can chart the insights and ideas that are most relevant to you.

It won't take long for you to discover the deeper rewards of the game and learn the lessons of the many EALs playing in every conceivable setting. I'm excited to introduce you to these leaders in the chapters ahead and share their lessons in hopes that they will inspire you, just as they have inspired me.

PART I
THE GAME

The defining characteristic of long-term success in business and life is recognizing the game and framing it as an energizing opportunity. Naming and framing your game helps you to quickly tap your available skills, knowledge, and talent to respond effectively to new challenges and opportunities. Understanding the elements of the game lights the path to leadership success. Through the chapters and coaching sections in Part I, you will discover how to identify the most compelling elements of your game, the "What" as well as your "Why" (your purpose), and begin to chart your "How" (clearing your pathway of obstacles). Using the Embodied Reflection and Action Framework, you will also learn how to make the most of the experiences and lessons you will discover throughout the book.

CHAPTER 1

WHAT IS THE GAME?

Discovering Your Four Ps

The avalanche hold on the steep and icy championship alpine racecourse had been released, but I was still convincing myself that I was ready to be at the start gate. As a flatlander from Chicago, I was still adjusting to the mountain altitude and my heart was pounding. I knew this was more than altitude. This was panic. I tried to slow my breathing and pull more oxygen into my lungs. Despite my efforts, my smartwatch started buzzing and blaring an alarm just as my age group was called. The watch, buried deep inside my race suit, was yet another stressor in an already stressful situation. I later learned that because my heart was pounding so hard when I was standing still, my watch thought I was having a heart attack and sent emergency alerts to my wife and the local sheriff.

Simultaneously, the woman before me pushes out of the start gate. I can tell from her first few turns that she is skiing somewhat tentatively. I feel a small wave of confidence as I slip in and position my poles over the timing wand. I can do this. The race official radioed down, "I have number 448 on yellow course." Before I fully realized that he was talking about me, I hear, "Yellow course, go!"

There is no time to regroup, no time to review my strategy. I remember the encouragement from my race coach friend, who texted me the night before to "Take chances!" Fueled by adrenaline, I push off.

Playing the Game When the Stakes Are High

Chances are you have encountered your share of stretch challenges, unexpected and unplanned events, and opportunities in your life and work. Most likely, your response to these occurrences has ranged from panic to excitement and everything in between. As each of us takes on new challenges and negotiates inevitable changes, our ability to find new possibilities and growth within them has a lot to do with our ability to name, frame, and claim our energy source.

> **As each of us takes on new challenges and negotiates inevitable changes, our ability to find new possibilities and growth within them has a lot to do with our ability to name, frame, and claim our energy source.**

You have also likely experienced a time in your career when big changes and new business goals were announced. At such times, you may have even seen this type of leadership in action: before the expected pushback to the changes gathers much steam, a few rare leaders respond entirely differently. Rather than resist changes, they are energized by them and quickly begin offering ideas and sharing resources to support the success of those changes. Perhaps you contributed to this positive momentum. By learning to identify the game, you can ensure you don't leave your positive response to new challenges to chance.

> If you want to understand
> organizations, study something else.[1]
> —**Karl Weick, Professor Emeritus, University of Michigan**

Working with leaders and studying high-stakes organizations, I have found wisdom in Karl Weick's claim that some of our best lessons and insights come from outside our familiar worlds. When leaders are in the thick of their latest challenge or opportunity, getting perspective and tapping fresh insights is almost impossible. Many leaders even struggle for insight during all-too-rare retrospective sessions. Happily, increasing numbers of case studies and research projects are probing organizations and human systems whose livelihood depends on their ability to learn and adapt in rapidly changing, high-stakes conditions. For example, in my book *From Workplace to Playspace*,[2] I shared some of these lessons from people learning to improvise (and professional improv teams) that can be practiced in other highly collaborative, high-stakes business situations. These lessons, along with research on such disparate groups as SWAT teams, film crews,[3] and wildfire fighters[4] are useful in helping us better understand how we can be effective in less dire yet still stressful challenges when things do not go as planned.

Playing With Embodied Agile Leadership

The kind of leadership I have witnessed in highly engaged people in varied terrains on and beyond the mountain is particularly relevant to today's VUCA environment (volatile, uncertain, complex, and ambiguous). Now widely used, the term VUCA was first coined by the US Army War College to describe rapidly changing conditions on the battlefield. These conditions call for a level of self-awareness and embodied presence often overlooked in traditional conceptions of leadership; they call for Embodied Agile Leaders, or EALs.

Rather than be defined by who or what they have power *over*, EALs have the power *to effect* positive change and make things happen. To be effective, EALs know they must engage their whole person and whole body, not just from the neck up, because today's conditions demand readiness and responsiveness like never before. This is the kind of leader that agile and innovative organizations know they must recruit and retain because their success depends on it.

Embodied Agile Leadership begins with self-leadership, although it certainly doesn't end there because we all know success doesn't happen in a vacuum. Such leadership enables us to be effective and responsive through varied terrain and shifting life and business conditions. EALs are resilient in the face of setbacks and quickly turn unplanned challenges into innovative opportunities.

It will be helpful to keep the image of the interconnected qualities of EALs in mind as you discover the intentional practice of Embodied Agile Leadership through the many examples and first-hand accounts throughout this book.

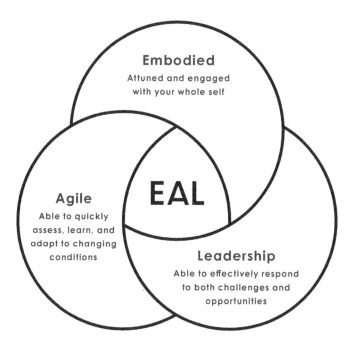

Countless EALs from all walks of life know their ability to learn and adapt to stay in the game is too important to be left to chance.

Given that individual, team, and organizational success starts with our first responses to disruption, it's shocking how often this aspect of performance goes unaddressed. That first response either taps the energy, talent, and creativity of individuals and teams or is overtaken by the primal forces of resistance to any threat to the status quo. If you cannot trust your ability or that of your colleagues to be effective amid disruption, pressure, and uncertainty, how can you be confident that you can sustain success over the long haul? EALs have a unique ability to find opportunities within disruption and change. They have learned to appreciate the energizing game within VUCA.

The Four Ps of the Game

The first step to tapping this energy is understanding the elements of *your* game. Think about your peak experiences of childhood play. Very likely, at least some of the scenarios that come to mind involved imaginary worlds that you and your friends brought to life—whether you played with store-bought items, such as a board game or video console, or you played in the great outdoors with found objects or on playground equipment. At their best, these games involve adventure and high stakes or at least some degree of chance and unpredictability. Not knowing how the game would end was the biggest part of the fun! As we move into adulthood with its many responsibilities and real-life consequences, unpredictability and chance lose their luster for most of us. It is possible, however, to reignite the game's energy while fostering the stability necessary to sustain our well-being and livelihood. Your participation in the game can even reinforce stability while building your confidence to turn unexpected challenges into exciting opportunities.

What endures from the less consequential games of childhood to the often more serious (but hopefully not *too* serious) games of adulthood are the "four Ps" of the game: play, purpose, passion, and pleasure.

THE GAME
- Play
- Purpose
- Passion
- Pleasure

- **Play:** Play provides opportunities for us to explore and experiment with possibilities on our way to becoming our best selves. It includes a chance to play with new ideas and roles and an opportunity for improvised play and creating more play in the system.[1] This kind of play, just like the play of our youth, is energizing, creative, and, at its best, fun.
- **Purpose:** Play can be both free-form and purposeful. Because our game has intrinsic meaning, we play with intention, whether for the reward of playing itself or for a valued outcome. In this way, playing also feeds our sense of purpose.
- **Passion:** To succeed in the game, we must engage wholeheartedly and with our whole selves—we must be passionate about it! When we are, we engage all our available resources to make the most of the present moment and achieve our aspirations.
- **Pleasure:** We are drawn to the game for a combination of intrinsic and extrinsic rewards that bring us joy and fuel our desire to continue to play.

The Four Ps in Action

These four elements of play keep people like Carol Taylor, Director of Training at one of the world's largest commuter rail lines, thriving in a decades-long career that has cycled between the public and private sectors. In each new role, Carol taps into her prior experience and brings her enthusiasm for learning and innovating as she explores new technologies and strategies. "I see it as a playground," she reflected, "Each new opportunity is a chance to learn and play with new ideas—for both them [the employees and learners] and me!" Taylor never rests on her formidable laurels but boldly jumps into new arenas.

For example, when she and her team were constrained by available time and money for new training initiatives, she was an early adopter of virtual simulated environments to provide experiential learning opportunities that were otherwise out of reach.

Through the years, I have enjoyed watching Carol in action and collaborating with her on an advisory board at DePaul University. No matter the context, her ability to play with passion and purpose never wavers. In a recent conversation, she enthusiastically told me about innovations she was experimenting with for more impactful learning in her high-stakes and highly regulated environment. Only months away from retirement, Carol was innovating until her last day on the job. But not without identifying her next playground in early retirement: learning to code.

Some leaders are tempted to dismiss the notion of play as superficial in business. Taylor and many other EALs demonstrate each day that there is nothing more serious than the deep engagement of leaders who are intrinsically motivated to lead through learning and exploration. These leaders stand out because organizational or industry constraints do not limit them. They boldly push into new territories, embrace new perspectives, and set aside their egos and need for personal validation for a greater purpose: the success of their colleagues, customers, and community.

Playing With Discomfort

Play, purpose, passion, and pleasure are not achieved by staying in your comfort zone or refusing to explore anything that disrupts it. Instead, any game worth playing stretches and challenges us. Why would we play if we already knew what was going to happen and how we were going to get there? The uncertainty many struggle with in business is the most engaging and fun part of the game. Unfortunately, those who resist change also resist engaging in the excitement of discovery as the game unfolds. Those who can only see negatives in changes and respond with fear forget this. When fear takes hold, rather than receive news of changes as an invigorating challenge, they respond as if the changes are an existential threat. Very likely, their bodies signal the alarm first, and their minds quickly follow. By naming and framing your game, you will be able to embody a positive response when the alarm bells of uncertainty and discomfort sound.

Naming and Claiming *YOUR* Game

You might name and claim (or reclaim) your game as you think about the four Ps of play, purpose, passion, and pleasure, as I did on my recent "big" birthday. Milestones such as these and significant disruptions or life changes often provoke us to reflect on existential questions such as, "Am I living my best life?" "Am I making an impact?" and "How could I be better and do better?"

Such questions invite you to look for patterns of engagement. For example, as I did with alpine skiing and racing, you might have first experienced the four Ps on the playing fields of your youth or another endeavor from your past.

> When I'm racing, I'm trying to go fast and carve turns, it just feels wonderful to me. It's like a soul massage.
> —James (J.C.) Black, 80-year-old ski racer, describing his game

Your game(s) might also include your peak experiences in your work. For me, I experience the four Ps during collaboration and co-creation with highly engaged, smart, creative professionals from various industries. I also experience them when I venture out of my comfort zone with colleagues to learn, explore, and experiment with new ideas and possibilities, developing new competencies and confidence. The four Ps also keep me in the game in my volunteer and board work in a youth arts and education program, collaborating with other business leaders to develop strategies and identify resources to fulfill our organization's mission.

There is no limit to the number of settings in which you experience and engage in your four Ps. The game may change over time, and you may choose to change the game or move on to entirely new playing fields. The only important thing is that you desire to get in and stay in compelling and energizing experiences.

Playing with Embodied Presence

At the top of that icy, giant slalom course, my body responded to the challenge and uncertainty with a racing heart, sending my smartwatch into a frenzy of alarms and text messages. At the same time, the challenge compelled me and my fellow racers to be there in the first place. Otherwise, we could have just submitted our handicaps from the season and waited for our medals to arrive. The exhilaration and fun came from negotiating the course conditions, our physical and mental strengths and limitations, and myriad other variables within and outside our control on race day. I won that day, not because I had the best handicap in my division going in or because I was the most experienced or best racer. I certainly was not. I believe I won that day, on a steeper course than I had ever raced, because I was able to shift my mindset from panic to playing with embodied presence.

I did not ignore my racing heart or need for more oxygen; I paid attention to it and transformed my embodied experience into a heightened presence that ultimately enabled my winning performance. Without this embodied awareness, there would have been nothing to access and nothing to transform. This is the value and purpose of naming and framing your game. It enables you to appreciate and embrace the challenge and opportunity, engaging your whole self and for your whole life.

COACHING
Name, Frame, and Claim Your Game

Of course, before you can play your game, you must be aware of when you are in it. This is not a one-time activity; your game and what gives you the four Ps may well evolve and shift as you do. Some of the best coaching I have received in my work and on the mountain help me reflect on my own experience and use the lessons I find as a guide for continued success. In this spirit, I encourage you to use the reflection prompts below to get started on the coaching in this chapter. Ideally, invite a friend or colleague to have this conversation with you. As you share your experiences and hear your friend's, you will gain even more clarity on the most compelling aspects of your game.

Download the *Embodied Reflection and Action Journal* with all of the coaching prompts, as well as additional resources here: https://pamela-meyer.com/staying-in-the-game-resources/ or use the QR code on the left.

Think about times when you experience some combination of the four Ps (play, purpose, passion, and pleasure) in your life and work.

- What are you feeling during these times? Be as specific and detailed as possible, including your emotions and physical sensations.
- What are you thinking?
- What are you (and others) doing?

- What capabilities (skills, knowledge, talents) are you demonstrating?
- Where/when else do you (or might you) experience this kind of engagement and fun in your life and work?

With these reflections as a starting point, draft a description of yourself at the height of your game and what you know so far about your four Ps. Include any characteristics of the context (people, place, etc) you experience being in your game. Keep this description close at hand; we'll return to it in the next chapter, where you will discover more about the value of staying in the game through Embodied Agile Leadership.

CHAPTER 2

WHY STAY IN THE GAME?

Leading and Learning with Your Embodied Agile Self

One evening Zaki Djemal brought together a group of Jewish and Muslim friends who had agreed to meet to generate ideas for an event for their communities to celebrate their shared love of Middle Eastern music. In a short time, Zaki felt the tension in the room develop into a heated debate that threatened to derail the project altogether.

An Israeli entrepreneur, Zaki founded the venture capital firm FreshFund in Jerusalem. I learned how he played the game with Embodied Agile Leadership when we started talking on a chairlift ride one morning in Winter Park, Colorado. Zaki was attending a conference in Denver and jumped at the chance to take the famous Winter Park Express ski train for a day on the mountain. We ended up skiing together the rest of the day, swapping stories and discovering many shared connections and interests.

He shared more about how the evening unfolded in the heated atmosphere of his friend's living room. Someone less present in their bodies and in the moment might have been reactive or defensive and decided to abandon the conversation and ideal of improved relations between people of widely divergent backgrounds, experiences, and perspectives. Zaki was able to pause and pay attention to what was going on in the room while holding his initial plan lightly. When one friend suggested they take a break and maybe even play a game together, Zaki quickly agreed. What some might have felt was too risky, he saw as an opportunity to experiment with a novel strategy.

Why Wouldn't You Want to Stay in the Game?

For EALs (Embodied Agile Leaders) like Zaki, who know the energy, engagement, and new learning the game offers, the question is, "Why *wouldn't* you want to stay in the game?" If you have found your way to a livelihood that integrates your life and work, or better yet, a way of being that engages your sense of play, provides you with purpose, taps your passion, and gives you pleasure, why would you want to *stop*?[1] When I put it this way, few argue with the value of finding, getting in, and staying in the game. At the same time, we all know the chasm that can exist between reality and our aspirations. The comfort of the known keeps us in unhealthy relationships, unfulfilling jobs, and unrewarding and sometimes destructive habits until we can no longer ignore the toll they are taking.

Valuing Disruption

Disruption, as uncomfortable as it can be, can serve a valuable purpose: shaking us out of our familiar mindset and routines to explore new possibilities. The COVID-19 pandemic did just this for countless people across the globe. In a study by the Society of Human Resource Management, in the United States alone, only 21% of workers reported being highly engaged. More than 50% planned to look for a new job as things started opening up.[2] These findings soon became a reality in the wave of job transitions known as "the great resignation."

The pandemic disrupted when, how, where, and even why we work, not to mention the actual work many of us do, igniting a period not only of re-evaluation but also re-valuation. For many people, this was a gift of the pandemic years. It gave them the spark to reevaluate and rediscover the importance of working and living in ways that honor and engage their whole selves.

The rapid shift to remote work for a large part of the working population; a heightened focus on family, health, and well-being; and a high demand for talent caused many to reconsider if their current livelihood was as lively as possible. The disruption posed clarifying questions: Could I have more meaningful experiences in which my skills, knowledge, and talent are engaged? Could I have more flexibility to continue learning and growing while also positively impacting something I truly care about? Could I be engaging in more rewarding relationships and communities? Answering these questions takes more than casual reflection; it takes Embodied Agile Leadership and the inspiration to (re)discover and (re)commit to playing your game.

Embodied Agile Leadership in Action

While uncomfortable for Zaki, the unexpected shift in energy and rising tension in the room became an opportunity to play with a new idea that was not part of the original plan but certainly worth exploring. As it happened, backgammon, the only game the hosts had on hand, was also the perfect game for the group. Backgammon, an age-old game that originated in the Middle East, is perhaps the only one known well by both Arab and Jewish people. Reflecting on that night, Zaki shared, "We didn't have any bigger plans other than playing. As we started playing, all of this tension we felt in the discussion was suddenly diffused. The original debate was forgotten. We saw there was real power in playing a game."[3]

If Zaki had approached the evening and his project from a traditional model of leadership, one focused solely on accomplishing the original goal, he might have stopped there. However, because he was *embodying* agile leadership, he was present to the deeper experience of what was happening in the room. Zaki had not brought his friends together to complete a transaction; he brought them together in hopes of fostering connection and maybe even transformation. Because of his ability to be present to the power of the moment that night, he asked himself, "[If] this is working so effectively with us, why not scale and expand it? That's how the idea was born. It's moved from that living room and involved thousands of people."[4]

Unleashing the Generative Power of Embodiment

EALs have an uncanny ability to stay with their "what if…" questions and commit time and resources to their experiments with sometimes unimaginable results. The spontaneous game that night has expanded to the nonprofit organization Kulna Yerushalayim, which Zaki founded. In a few short years, it has sponsored more than 10,000 Jewish-Arab encounters, among other initiatives to foster peace through understanding and relationship building.

The organization has continued to expand and adapt in response to the constraints of the pandemic and ever-shifting geopolitical tensions in the region. In response to COVID-19, the association's members began intensive assistance activities for the residents of East Jerusalem, including distributing food baskets to hundreds of needy families, visiting older individuals, and providing relief activities for children. For their impact through the mobilization of hundreds of volunteers, the association won the "President's Award for Volunteering" for 2021.[5]

EALs who engage with their whole, embodied, agile selves can discover how to get in and play the game because they know why they want to play in the first place. Leading with Embodied Agile Leadership enabled Zaki and his friends to discover the opportunity of the moment and play a literal game as they lived into their purpose and passion. Once unleashed, the generative energy of the group naturally expanded with even greater impact.

EALs respond positively by intentionally shifting their mindset and developing skills and habits that enable them to effectively respond to the unexpected and unplanned with curiosity and confidence. Those who have made the mindset shift see the unexpected as an exciting opportunity. They respond positively and quickly to understand the game at hand and the emerging possibilities within it. They collaborate with their colleagues to identify resources and generate ideas for implementing changes and achieving new goals while creating even more value for their stakeholders.

Embodying a Renewed Way of Being

Staying in the game is a way of *being* first and *doing* second. The agile leadership embodied by Zaki Djemal and others around the globe in boardrooms and living rooms brings to life the three interconnected dynamic states introduced in Chapter 1: embodiment, agility, and leadership.

Zaki's example beautifully illustrates the three interconnected practices of Embodied Agile Leadership. I refer to these as practices because they happen not accidentally but through intentional and repeated engagement and practice.

Embodiment

The practice of embodiment can be understood in two ways: 1) to *embody* a belief or quality is to bring it to life authentically and concretely, and 2) to be *embodied* is to be attuned and engaged with your whole self, as well as within your current context. In much of Western and business culture, we are discouraged from embodying our whole physical, emotional, and spiritual selves, let alone bringing this whole self to work. Yet, when we engage with our whole selves and learn to think with what some call our three brains—head, heart, and gut[6]—we can be more effective, particularly in high-stakes situations. Embodied awareness enabled Zaki and his friends to discern the signals from their reactive reptilian brains[7]—the part of the brain responsible for self-preservation—to keep them from venturing outside the comfort of their caves.[8] Embodied awareness gave them access to insight, creativity, energy, and motivation that were critical to their success.

Agility

People are born with agility, the innate capacity to experiment, learn, and adapt. It is the key to our survival. Zaki also embodied another aspect of agility: the ability to respond effectively to the unexpected and unplanned and quickly turn challenges into opportunities.[9] To be effective in a complex world that often defies rationality, we must practice engaging our whole selves to embody agility.

Leadership

The practice of Embodied Agile Leadership is grounded in self-awareness and self-leadership. For this reason, an EAL can be anyone who becomes aware of a challenge or opportunity and effectively responds through learning and adaptation. EALs may also lead in authoritative ways or more collaboratively, depending on how they assess the needs of the current context.

Discerning the best approach for the moment requires Embodied Agile Leadership. For this reason, it is both a practice and a *renewed* way of being. It is not a new way of being, so much as one we need to intentionally renew, often many times a day. This intentionality is necessary because of the ingrained pull to prioritize the original plan. We have been well trained to value completing the day's checklist or accomplishing our short-term goals despite new information that signals the futility of staying the course. Embodied Agile Leadership encourages us to be aware of and adapt to the current reality, even if it wasn't in our original plan. It also allows us to prioritize our values and the value we generate and deliver when the situation changes. This way of being and leading requires and invites renewal and integration.

Sustaining a true agility shift requires a significant and enduring mindset shift and a new way of leading. It means leadership practices that *embody* the whole self and are fueled by continuous learning and adapting as conditions change. This is Embodied Agile Leadership.

Making the Agility Shift

Leaders who make these intentional shifts do so because they recognize the need to be present in and attuned to their bodies and their environment. For example, the leaders who can shift from resisting disruption to generating innovative solutions are present enough to be aware of what is happening in the room (organization, market, community) and in their own bodies. They are aware of their temptation to follow the guidance of their hard-wired threat-averse brains and to pause long enough to make an agility shift.

My racing heart at the top of that icy giant slalom course gave me the opportunity to make such a shift. My blaring smartwatch alarm was not a signal to abandon the competition but to gather my full presence and confidence in a challenging situation. These, and countless stories of success in high-stakes situations, all begin with embodied presence. Western culture—particularly Western business culture—prioritizes action. Of course, business success depends on not just any action but *effective* action.

Embodied Agile Leadership Is Not Optional

Embodied Agile Leadership was not optional for me at the top of the icy racecourse any more than it was for Zaki in a potentially tense evening of community-building or for business leaders who make the intentional shift from resistance to resourcefulness in the face of change.

Our experience of personal fulfillment and impact, as well as every business or organization's success, depends on its ability to be present, engage, learn, and adapt to ever-changing conditions. Even the US Postal Service, which used to be held up as a possible exception, must now adapt to compete with other carriers. Today, agile leaders in every sector, industry, and business must keep their fingers on the pulse of changing demographics, customer and market needs, social trends, scientific and technological advances, geopolitical and natural climates, and more.

COACHING
Finding Your Why

The reasons to renew your approach to the game through Embodied Agile Leadership and your reasons for wanting to stay in it will be as unique as you are. The intrinsic value of the game itself or your experience of yourself while playing it, as you described based on Chapter 1's coaching, may be enough. This is the case for many masters athletes and business leaders I studied. It might well be the people themselves and the energy and engagement you feel by participating. Or your driver might be attaining a sought-after goal. Very likely, it is some combination of each of these.

At these times, your "why?" can serve as both a touchstone and motivator. Rather than taking for granted your purpose for staying in the game, clarifying your personal "why?" in writing can help you stay engaged and persevere as you encounter the inevitable setbacks or obstacles. Give yourself the gift of slowing down enough to follow these few prompts to get to your game's root and describe its value. I promise that you will make up the time you take now when life and work speed up, as you know they will, and you need to make shift happen quickly and effectively.

Download the *Embodied Reflection and Action Journal* with all of the coaching prompts, as well as additional resources here: https://pamela-meyer.com/staying-in-the-game-resources/ or use the QR code on the left.

Start by re-reading your description of yourself at your best from the Chapter 1 coaching.

- Ask yourself, "Why is that important to me?"
- In response to your answer, again ask, "Why is that important to me?" and respond up to five times or until you think you have identified your most compelling "why?"

Example:

At my best, I feel present and energized while interacting with other creative and engaged individuals. I am constantly learning and being challenged to grow.

"Why is that important to me?"

Because when I am learning and growing, I improve my ability to perform and make a difference.

"Why is that important to me?"

Because I want to engage and inspire others to live and work at the top of their talent, and I can only do that if I challenge myself to do the same.

"Why is that important to me?"

Because I believe the world is a better place when more people are developing their full capabilities and living and working at the top of their talent.

Keep your "Five Why"[10] responses handy. They can remind you why you are staying in the game in the first place and help restore your passion when things don't go as planned—which they won't. In the next chapter, you will learn more about how those staying in the game assess and overcome barriers that keep many from ever getting in the game in the first place.

CHAPTER 3

WHAT'S STOPPING YOU?

Realistically Assessing Risks and Reaping Rewards

Feel it. Know what it is. Go do it.
—Dick Cole, 83-year-old alpine ski racer

A recent ad campaign promoting tourism in Illinois asks, "When was the last time you tried something for the first time?" The campaign is effective. Against a rolling montage of happy families, friends, and couples zip-lining, rock climbing, walking into a history museum, and listening to jazz, the ad entices us to break out of our comfort zone for a new experience—preferably in Illinois, but who's counting?

Most people have something they would like to try for the first time or do differently than they have done before. But something holds them back. This "something" is often fear—not necessarily the heart-pounding, run-for-your-life kind of fear but the fear that masquerades as resistance or sometimes inertia. When it comes to trying something new, the purpose of this resistance is to avoid risk (real or imagined) and keep us in our comfort zone. The trouble is that the comfort zone is not a zone of high engagement, learning, or growth. Comfort is not one of the four Ps of the game. Why? Because experiences that move us forward are often uncomfortable. Embodied Agile Leaders (EALS) recognize the power that resistance can have over themselves and their colleagues. For this reason, EALs do not seek their comfort zone. They practice becoming comfortable with being uncomfortable.

> **EALs do not seek their comfort zone. They practice becoming comfortable with being uncomfortable.**

Knowing and Negotiating Your Barriers

As uncomfortable as they may be, new experiences and the play, purpose, passion, and pleasure they create are also exhilarating, energizing, and restorative. They can also be disruptive and risky because their very newness brings uncertainty and the discomfort of the unfamiliar. EALs do not so much *overcome* these obstacles but instead learn about them and how to negotiate them.

Understanding and confronting your barriers is the first step to moving beyond them. EALs are masters at assessing the risks and rewards of exhilarating new territory. I've learned some important lessons about risk assessment from masters racers and from working with leaders of some of the world's largest insurance companies and other highly regulated industries. These leaders inevitably start our conversation on agility by emphasizing that they are very risk-averse. At the same time, they recognize that they must be agile to stay competitive and meet the changing needs of their customers. While I've yet to work with a successful organization that did not have a healthy relationship with risk, I've learned some valuable insights from those whose business is to insure against unexpected and unplanned losses.

Balancing Risk and Reward

Success comes to those who understand how to minimize risk and maximize value. EALs balance risk and reward in a way that respects the consequences of possible failure while not missing out on the significant benefits of success. As a leader, your job is to strike this balance without becoming paralyzed in endless analysis.

> **Embodied Agile Leaders are attuned to themselves and their current reality and can learn and adapt to respond effectively to challenges and opportunities.**

The barriers that can either hold us back or derail us from staying in the game fall into three broad categories: physical, financial, and social-emotional, along with a fourth bonus category I call the "what if…" barriers. EALs know they must be aware of these barriers and assess whether they are worth addressing or are just another attempt by the reptilian brain to keep them from venturing out of familiar territory.

Physical Risk

One of the reasons I have used skiing as a metaphor throughout this book is because it holds a real risk of injury. For many people, this possibility, however unlikely, is enough to keep them from even giving it a try. Slowing down to assess the actual likelihood of physical risk and your comfort with it can ensure you don't miss out on the rewards of your game. No guarantees are expressed or implied here. If you need a reminder of your limited ability to eliminate all physical risks, just ask the woman who stayed home from the family ski trip because she thought it was too dangerous and then broke her hip slipping on a patch of black ice in her driveway, taking out the trash!

EALs do not operate with the illusion of eliminating physical risk. Instead, they acknowledge it and prepare. It would be foolhardy and arrogant not to. For example, my ski-racing friends and I reduce our risk by training during the off-season, ensuring our equipment is in good order, and adapting to conditions on the day of the event. We are (hopefully) wise enough to abort the mission up to the start time if the conditions are too treacherous or beyond our ability. Others adapt if they feel less than confident or if the physical risk outweighs their enjoyment of a particular event. For example, one woman realized that when she was in the start gate for giant slalom races, she was thinking, "How can I go faster?" But when positioned at the top of slalom courses, facing a daunting string of gates that were more tightly set (meaning less time to turn), her thought was, "I hope I don't die." That was all she needed to shift her energy into the game she wanted to play and stick with giant slalom.

In the unfortunate event of injury, we mediate the consequences through contingency plans and a strong network of fellow players whom we can trust to help us get the immediate care we need. Even if the likelihood of serious physical injury in your game is relatively low, it is worth assessing and adapting to be sure you are set up for success. Developing creative strategies to reinforce your networks, develop contingencies, and train in your metaphorical off-season can greatly reduce risk, with the added benefit of increasing engagement.

Financial Risk

When confronted with change, new opportunities, or the prospect of embarking on a new adventure, many of us must face the fear of financial loss or uncertainty. New endeavors often demand new investments; any change can disrupt the financial status quo. You might ask, "What if I get downsized out of my job?" or "How might this move burden my family?" or "If things don't work out, how will I provide for myself and my family?" or "What other financial stability is at risk if I take on this new challenge or opportunity?"

Thinking and feeling your way through the possible risks and benefits is one way to determine your readiness for the game's rewards. It might ease your mind to follow the lead of the risk-averse insurance industry. They assess risks that fall into two key areas: absolute and speculative.

- **Absolute risks** are those in which the risk of a loss is not offset by a possible gain, such as personal risks and risks to our property, flood, fire, theft, medical emergency, etc. It would be nearly impossible, not to mention life constraining, to avoid such risks altogether (e.g., to choose not to own any property or not move about in the world in any meaningful way). Most of us mediate absolute risk with various best practices (e.g., not leaving burning candles unattended or our office unlocked and following industry compliance and regulatory guidelines).
- **Speculative risk** is a risk that has exposure to possible losses but also benefits or gains that can far outweigh the risk. We speculate that the companies we invest in will grow and be profitable. We speculate that our relationships will be generative, meaningful, and rewarding. We speculate that the new opportunities we pursue will be well worth the disruption they cause our loved ones and us. In business, we also speculate that our investments in employees, new technology, expansion into new markets, and new product and service lines will yield returns many times over.

In our personal and business lives, we do our best to assess the cost-benefit, or potential return on investment, against the possibility of loss. We might seek outside advisors, run complex analyses, trust our gut, or rely on some combination of all three. After all, it is a risk because there is no guarantee of success.[1]

Just as athletes reduce their physical risk and overcome barriers through rigorous training and preparation, successful assessment and preparation are key to balancing financial risk and reward. Individuals and businesses must be aware of and attend to their exposure to absolute risks. For example, individuals may create backup plans, financial cushions, or other contingencies. At the same time, businesses mitigate financial risk by carrying appropriate insurance, practicing good safety habits, creating business continuity plans, and providing proper training. Individual EALs and their organizations also develop cost-savings analyses for new initiatives that diversify revenue sources and dilute exposure when inevitable setbacks occur.

Social-Emotional Risks

In my experience working with leaders across industries and with adult university students, I have found that social-emotional risks can be the most daunting to overcome. Often without our full awareness, the fear of being rejected, looking silly (at best), or incompetent (at worst) keeps us from venturing into new territory and experiences. Unfortunately, it also keeps us from learning new skills we need to stay relevant and competitive. David Rock, director of the Neuro-Leadership Institute, has identified five social-emotional fears that can hold us back from full engagement and peak performance, using the acronym SCARF.[2]

- **Status:** fear of looking bad or losing credibility

    This is essentially the classic fear of not being good enough or looking stupid. New experiences and opportunities often require new skills and demand that we participate in new and unfamiliar ways. Whether it's a new role in a familiar context or a new context altogether, our success depends on our ability to learn and adapt. That learning process is not always comfortable or outwardly pretty. We likely won't look entirely competent at the start and may even feel stupid. This social anxiety alone is a barrier enough to stop many people in their tracks and send them back to their familiar if unengaging, endeavors.

- **C**ertainty: fear of the unknown

   The brain hates uncertainty. We are wired to constantly assess the environment for threats and then work to avoid them at all costs. Unfortunately, this means avoiding new experiences that stretch our capacity and imagination and challenge us to continue to grow.

- **A**utonomy: fear of losing personal agency

   If you have ever resisted a group vacation or tour because you wanted to be in control of your schedule or experiences, you understand this barrier. The good news is that more and more workplaces, educational institutions, and tour companies understand this barrier to engagement and are providing more customized options. Appreciating that you need some degree of autonomy over your experience can boost your courage to ask for or create that experience. However, I also caution you not to miss out on a new experience or opportunity just because, at first, it seems constraining. Despite my initial resistance, some of my favorite adventures in work and travel have involved being herded onto buses, trains, planes, and boats to experience new sites, new learning, and new people.

- **Relatedness:** fear of losing connectedness and belongingness to the group

    This is the fear of not belonging or not being welcomed and is directly related to the fear of looking or feeling stupid. It is even more foundational. As much as we have a primal need to avoid threats, we also have a primal need to belong. Our survival as a species from our earliest days has depended on our acceptance into and survival of a group. Within a group, we have access to shared resources, greater physical safety, the possibility of forming intimate relationships, and mutual support to experience life and achieve goals that we could not reach on our own. This barrier has a powerful antidote: the co-creation and participation in Community. You will discover how EALs find and sustain Community in Chapter 5.

- **Fairness:** fear of not being treated equitably

    The fifth of David Rock's social-emotional barriers is at the heart of diversity, equity, and inclusion (DEI) programs. You don't need to attend a workshop to know that it is impossible to feel included and valued if you don't believe you are being treated fairly and equitably. And why would you want to play a game if the rules did not seem to apply equally to all players? It's human nature to assess any new endeavor for fairness. Are all people welcomed and included equally? Are new opportunities available to all? If compensation, promotion, recognition, or rewards are involved, are they based on unbiased decision-making? Knowing the answers to these questions will free you to fully commit to the game with confidence that you and your fellow players will enjoy its rewards equally.

These social-emotional fears can trigger a full-out threat response from the part of the brain designed to protect us from danger. But it turns out that the brain has a hard time differentiating between social risks and risks that are indeed life or death because they can feel the same at the level of our emotions and bodies. This is not surprising because in our not-too-distant past as a species, being ostracized or separated from the group led to almost certain death.

Even if these fears are unfounded, or at least exaggerated, for most of us, in most contexts, our ability to be effective when social-emotional fear rears its head is a matter of perspective. We can minimize these fears by being aware of which one(s) are preventing us from getting in and staying in the game rather than keeping us safe. For example, I experienced a combination of status, certainty, and relatedness fears when I returned to skiing and ski racing after a 25-year hiatus. "What if I'm too old to learn and adapt to the new equipment?" "What if I look like an idiot?" "What if I can't find anyone to ski with, or I am not welcomed into the ski club?" Thankfully, I was able to become aware of and respond to those fears as they emerged. However, had I not been aware of them, put them into perspective, and forged ahead, I might still be pining for a mountain adventure and missing out on countless rewards and benefits.

What if . . . or "Fear of Flying" Barriers

The "what if…" barriers are a kind of "gift with purchase" because they include all the possible things that could "go wrong," as well as generalized free-floating anxiety. They can consist of elements of the physical and financial barriers but come to us courtesy of our friend, the reptilian brain. Because the job of this portion of our brain is to ensure our survival, it is known to make up wild stories of our spectacular demise before we even stick our metaphorical big toe in unfamiliar waters.

For example, even though most of us know that flying is by far the safest form of transportation, some people feel it is less risky to drive, despite the evidence.[3,4] This information usually doesn't help those with a debilitating fear of flying. It turns out that control, or rather, the illusion of control, gives people a greater sense of safety than actual safety. They feel much more comfortable with the control they feel behind the wheel of a car, even though their chances of death are much greater than the perceived lack of control in the air. These threats, unfortunately, do not always respond to disconfirming evidence, but it is still worth seeing if any evidence backs up our fears. Using reality as a starting point, we can look our free-floating fears in the eye and get support to move through them.

The Fear Paradox

One of my colleagues at DePaul University, instructional designer, amateur speed skater, trail runner, Canine Biathlon® competitor, and swim coach Melissa Koenig, related another interesting paradox of how fear can derail our success in the game.

> I've had this conversation with some of the other masters athletes when they tell me they are afraid of getting hurt and say things like, "I've got two kids in college. At the end of

the day, I have to go to work tomorrow." And I say to them, "The more scared you are to race or skate, the more likely you are to get hurt." I also used to teach swimming lessons to adults, and the more fearful they were, the more tense they were, and the more they struggled to float. You will not float if you are tense. You will sink to the bottom of the pool.

For many EALs, swimming is an apt metaphor for the new and often turbulent waters they must tread. Too rigid and they are sure to sink; too relaxed and they may fail to notice the coming squall. Neurologic hardwiring makes us pay more attention to negative feedback and the possibility of adverse outcomes than to positive ones.[5]

Negativity bias served us well when threats from predators and strangers in our midst often signaled that we might be on the brink of a life-and-death battle. It does not serve us well today when most of our "threats" involve things like needing to make decisions quickly in response to an opportunity, such as moving into a new role, investing in emerging technology, building a relationship with someone very different from ourselves, learning a new skill, or living or working in a different culture. Sometimes the most effective action is to slow down long enough to take a deep breath and return to the present moment. An intentional breath or two is just enough time to realistically assess our current situation and shift our bodies from reactive to responsive.

As you take that breath, you might also take an extra step to shift your negativity bias toward positivity with something psychologists call cognitive reappraisal. For example, rather than giving in to the fear of looking foolish or of failing, positively reframe it as a possibility. What if you are welcomed with open arms and cheered on as you build your competence and confidence in your new endeavor? What if you did the same for others taking new risks? Imagine that.

What Will It Cost You NOT to Stay in the Game?

In addition to becoming aware of and realistically assessing risk, you may confront another obstacle. You may simply miss the spark you need to explore new territory. Or perhaps *you* are motivated but are searching for ways to spark *others* to get in the game.

Whether you need the spark or are looking to spark others, I've discovered some excellent strategies for helping leaders who are struggling to engage broader support for Agile transformations and other disruptive changes in their organizations. First, I remind them of the old saying that everyone listens to the same radio station: WIIFM (What's In It For Me?). The trick is to find out what station your leaders are listening to. Is it employee engagement? Market share? Number of patents filed? Customer loyalty? Shareholder value? What success indicators do they care about and to which are they held accountable? Helping others understand the connection between embracing the game or other changes on the horizon and what they value can go a long way toward gaining more leadership support.

Making room for individuals to personalize the value of developing new capabilities and working through the discomfort of change can also enhance engagement. If you need help connecting the dots between developing new capabilities and business results, I detail some excellent research in *The Agility Shift*. With some attention, you can also identify the WIIFM for yourself and make space for your team to do the same.

However, sometimes making the business case is not enough to create the urgency to spur action. For example, I might flip the script and encourage leaders to consider, "What will it cost you NOT to become more agile and innovative?" Often this reflection prompts serious conversations about whether the current organizational mindset, strategies, systems, and processes will deliver competitive results 3, 5, 10, or more years from now. Just read your favorite daily business news source to hear about the latest industry titan struggling for survival because it did not take the threat or opportunity of changing technology, consumer habits, or social and economic trends seriously. For example, in Chicago, the business headlines declared the downfall of Sears, our iconic hometown company. The department store, founded in 1893, operated 3,500 stores just a decade ago. By 2022, its combined locations, including K-Mart stores, had shrunk to only 182 sites[6] with even fewer left by the time you read this.

Awareness of the possible cost of not adapting as the game changes can create an urgency to spark you to adapt and get back in the game. It works for Jimmy, the 84-year-old retired phone company worker I met my first year of ski racing camp—the camp I almost didn't attend for fear I would be the oldest racer. Jimmy inspires me for many reasons, most of which I discovered in conversations with him on a series of chairlift rides that week. I quickly learned that Jimmy's weekly fitness regimen puts mine to shame: daily hours-long workouts, followed by 3-mile walks, except on the weekends when he goes on 90-mile bike rides!

Not skiing, working out, walking, or riding is not an option for Jimmy. He knows the cost of not moving. He witnesses it each month when he meets with his retired buddies from the phone company, most of whom stay home and watch television all day. They are overweight, can barely move, and have aged dramatically in retirement; more than a few have passed away. Not Jimmy. For him, the cost of not moving is life or death. Simply put, he told me, "You stop skiing, you're dead." It's true. You stop moving, stop learning, stop growing, stop doing what you love, you are dead. Just ask Sears.

Just Saying "No!" Doesn't Work

Research shows that as effective as scare tactics can be in getting our attention about the urgent need for change, they are ineffective in the long run. Comprehensive studies by the American Heart Association confirm that fear is not the best motivator to change, at least regarding behavior changes. Case in point: heart disease is the #1 cause of death in the United States, while stroke-related death comes in at #5. In one large-scale study, researchers followed over 7,500 heart attack survivors in 17 countries. They found that even after a heart attack, 48% of smokers continued to smoke, 65% did not exercise, over 60% did not improve their diet, and 14% had not adopted one lifestyle improvement.[7] Even knowing they are already lucky to have survived because, for many, the first sign of heart disease is fatal cardiac arrest is not enough. Even with clear guidelines on ways that they can reduce their risk (such as stopping smoking,[8] losing weight, increasing exercise, and cutting back on alcohol use), a surprising percentage of survivors do not markedly change their behavior to reduce risk.

The heart disease study is a sobering reminder. It may save you from making the same mistake made by many leaders and the consultants who guide them: believing that if people are provided with compelling information, they will consider and respond with rational decisions, actions, and behavior changes. What fear-based approaches fail to account for is reality. Humans often don't make rational decisions in their personal lives or business. Researchers have confirmed that emotions and our current embodied state can heavily bias our decisions.[9,10] Additionally, we often subconsciously behave in ways and make heavily biased decisions to preserve our comfort, our current thinking, and the status quo.

Just Saying "Yes!" Does

Based on their research, behavioral scientists have a few helpful suggestions that can help us overcome our resistance to changes that may disrupt our comfort zone and transform fear into courage. All those "scared straight" and "Just Say No!" messages are not nearly as helpful in changing our behavior as tapping into our intrinsic motivation for a more positive experience or outcome. Behaviorists call attempts to motivate new behavior using fear as "avoidance" goals and those driven by a positive outcome as setting "approach" goals.[11] For example, research shows that instead of telling yourself, "I'm going to swim 30 minutes a day to avoid another heart attack," you will have more success telling yourself, "I'm going to swim 30 minutes a day to improve my health and energy."

Whether your initial spark to get in the game is to avoid a negative outcome or to inspire a dynamic future, staying in the game is almost always driven by intrinsic motivation—the love of the game itself and the engagement and possibilities you discover while playing. Intentional reflection will help you engage your intrinsic motivation and discover your WIIFM. Through reflection, you will also become aware of, assess, and overcome barriers that might keep you from getting in or staying in the game.

COACHING

Identifying and Assessing Your Risks and Rewards

The prompts below will help you to identify and assess the obstacles you may encounter in playing and staying in the game and to get ready to transform them into growth opportunities. In the next chapter, you will learn more about how to draw on this embodied reflection to help you transform your barriers into new opportunities using the *Embodied Reflection and Action Framework*.

Download the *Embodied Reflection and Action Journal* with all of the coaching prompts, as well as additional resources here: https://pamela-meyer.com/staying-in-the-game-resources/ or use the QR code on the left.

- What am I learning in response to the new information and examples so far?
- What am I feeling in response to my new learning? Which of these embodied responses is getting my attention?
- Which of my insights above are most relevant to my game (purpose, passion, pleasure, and ability to play)?
- What obstacles are getting in the way of my success?
- How can I or who/what can I engage to help remove these obstacles?
- What new habits or practices will help me sustain my progress?

CHAPTER 4

LEADING WITH LEARNING

Transforming Barriers into Growth Opportunities

Only a few years before the harrowing race I described in the opening chapters, I returned to ski racing after a more than twenty-year hiatus. It began during college when money and time for such activities were nonexistent. During the inevitable reflection that comes with birthdays ending in zero, I realized that the barriers that had kept me from a significant source of my four Ps were not as formidable as they once were; they had simply turned to inertia. To overcome this inertia and reclaim the game and the joy and exhilaration that came with it, I needed to make some significant and intentional shifts.

Humbling Lessons in Learning

My reclamation began with organizing a ski trip with friends to get reintroduced to the sport and all the equipment advances since I had last skied. That next winter, it took just a few impromptu runs on a public NASTAR racecourse[1] to be bitten by the racing bug again. Soon after, I sought out others who shared a passion for racing, joined a local ski club, and began participating in weekend races. After a few medals at Midwest races, I qualified for my first national championship in Snowmass, Colorado.

I arrived full of enthusiasm but short on experience. It didn't take long to discover that the other racers seemed to know much more about what they were doing than I did. They appeared more excited than nervous. They had coaches and race suits. They were *serious*. I was clearly out of my league, feeling like a stuffed sausage in my snow pants and ski jacket with my race bib pulled over the outside. In that first race, I came in last in my division.

I returned to Chicago humbled and more than a little embarrassed at my initial hubris and spectacular failure. Why had I thought I could compete without serious training, little preparation, and a limited and outdated understanding of the game? My delusions of grandeur were particularly ironic because my life's work is helping business leaders become more agile and innovative. This work has taught me that agile innovation and positive results don't happen accidentally. Of course, we all have stories of rising to the occasion during a crisis. Still, no leader or organization can sustain success over time without intentionally developing and practicing the skills, knowledge, and abilities to be effective through volatile and stable circumstances. Somehow, I had forgotten this in my early days of returning to the slopes.

Thankfully, after slowing down to reflect on my experience and consider my options, I took the advice I often give my clients when they encounter performance issues. I sought out opportunities to build my skills and confidence. This quest led me to Dave Gregory's Peak

Performance Race Camp at Copper Mountain, where for the first time I received individualized coaching and began to see my performance improve. Dave and his coaches are committed to providing "relentless positive feedback." This positivity builds racers' confidence, from which developmental feedback can take hold.

With an emphasis on leading with learning, each participant can transform their success barriers into growth opportunities. Each camp session includes real-time feedback at the bottom of each training run. Lunchtime video analysis of our runs allows us to recognize the gap between what we think we are doing and reality. We then receive more coaching and take our individual goals into afternoon drills to practice the skills we need to bring into the gates the next day. While I always have a breakthrough or two during the camp, the real value unfolds throughout the season when I pull out my little red notebook with each day's feedback to refocus and reinforce my progress. I know real learning is happening when I can embody the coaching and use it to adjust my performance in real time.

Understanding and Valuing Embodied Reflection

My humbling experience of returning to ski racing taught me to value not only reflection but *embodied* reflection. Such reflection shines new light on the internal and external barriers that might be getting in your way and gives you the power to transform them into opportunities for learning and growth. Reflecting with intention is critical because whether you went to business school or beauty school, or were simply raised in Western culture, you have been steeped in a mindset that prioritizes planning and control over learning and adaptation.

This outdated view is based on the belief that the more energy and attention we put into planning up front (which is when we know the least about our endeavor), the more we can reduce uncertainty and risk. The historical bias toward planning and control is based on two flawed assumptions: first, that the future is stable and knowable, and second, that we won't discover anything new about ourselves, our capabilities, or the current reality that might require us to change our minds or adapt as we execute the plan.

Embodied reflection enables Embodied Agile Leaders (EALs) to make the intentional shift from planning to preparing[2] and to have an iterative approach to their lives and work. This attuned mindset and practice shift do not happen by accident.

> **Trust your ability to learn and adapt, NOT your plan.**

As Product Group Manager at Netherlands-based FrieslandCampina Ingredients,[3] Abbie More has made the shift from planning to preparing throughout her career. In addition to leading a cross-functional team of scientists and product specialists in an ever-evolving arena, Abbie taps her experience moving through to the highest ranks of professional ski instructing and race coaching. The goal in both, she discovered, is not to ignore or be without fear when the stakes are high. She shared, "I have had several instances in my ski life when I've been terrified." The key is to realistically assess the barrier and transform it into an opportunity. Abbie had a breakthrough at the top of a particularly challenging run that has guided her success ever since. While trying out for the Development Team of the Professional Ski Instructors of America, the next level for advanced instructors, she shared:

> I saw a catwalk, and I thought, "I could just bail. This is too scary. This is too hard for me. What if I can't ski? What if I can't turn my feet? Let me just do that. Let me just take the easy way down, and we'll forget this ever happened." Then I said, "Yeah, right, and you look at yourself in the mirror tomorrow morning, and you'll be really disappointed. Just stop it and do it." I did, and nothing bad happened to me.
>
> I had an awesome run. I felt great about it. I got really good feedback, so I try and remind myself of challenging points like that when something was scary to me. It was a risk. Yeah, I had to put myself out there that day. Seven or eight examiners had their little cards in their hands, and they were watching me and taking notes. They were watching my every move, and I had to challenge myself to make a shift. Your head wants to say, "They're going to watch for mistakes." But I was able to turn that around and say, "They're going to watch for your good movements."

Assessing the situation through embodied reflection and shifting her mindset has translated into Abbie's leadership role. For example, when she delivers her quarterly report to the entire global organization, Abbie reminds herself, "You got this. You know what you're doing. They're not looking to you for mistakes. They're looking to you for information to help the organization. Just drawing from those experiences, turning my mindset around has really, really helped me get through some hard things, some challenging things."

Types of Embodied Reflection

For EALs like Abbie, embodied reflection means going beyond cognitive awareness and understanding. It is rooted in attunement to what is happening in the body and discerning the messages found there. For this reason, embodied reflection starts with embodied awareness. With awareness, we can learn and adapt to our current reality, often in the present moment. For example, if you have ever presented in front of a group and become aware of your mouth getting dry, your face flushing, and perhaps speaking so quickly you are running out of breath, you have experienced embodied awareness. With embodied reflection, you might have chosen to pause, catch your breath, and take a sip of water to regroup and reconnect with yourself and your audience. Without embodied awareness or reflection, you might have found yourself ignoring these signals and motoring on, missing the opportunity to make intentional shifts. Sometimes EALs make these shifts in the moment, such as Zaki did when he shifted his plan in the community meeting in Chapter 2. In other cases, embodied awareness and reflection provide critical feedback to inform everything from career shifts to shifts in business strategy, as you will see in the coming chapters.

Embodied reflection can be especially helpful for EALs who are leading with learning and have an intention or outcome in mind. Intentionality provides a focus so they can translate their embodied reflection into specific action, whether it be going faster, engaging an audience, or improving business results. As you become more intentional in your practice, you will find yourself using each of these four types of embodied reflection:

- **Anticipatory Reflection:** Before engaging in a new endeavor, EALs sometimes use their imagination to explore various scenarios. Rather than limit themselves to a purely "if-then" analysis, they imagine the fuller lived experience of possibilities. Some EALs incorporate this type of reflection as a kind of rehearsal for high-stakes endeavors so as not to be derailed when encountering intense embodied experiences in the heat of the moment. If you have ever found your heart racing, even thinking about stepping into a new frontier, you have engaged in this type of embodied reflection. These bodily sensations and emotions can provide valuable feedback as we discover the most engaging and fruitful pathways forward.
- **Reflecting in Action:** This type of embodied reflection happens in the present moment as the action is unfolding. It includes an awareness of bodily sensations (such as emotions, breath, heart rate, level of tension or relaxation), awareness of the body in space (stance/posture, balance, physical relationship to the environment and other people), as well as feedback from or response to the physical and/or social environment. Abbie practiced reflecting in action during her high-stakes evaluation on the mountain described earlier.
- **Reflecting-on-Action:** This is the most familiar type of reflection overall, though most of us struggle to make time to practice. Reflection-on-action means slowing down to look in the rearview mirror to celebrate successes and discover lessons learned. This type of reflection is so important to

agile success that the military has practiced it for generations in the form of After-Action Reviews, and Agile frameworks set aside time for formal Retrospective sessions. However, the traditional practice of Reflecting-on-Action tends to leave our bodies behind. EALs slow down enough to explore not just what worked and what needs improvement, but to appreciate what they and their colleagues were feeling. This type of reflection is critical for understanding levels of engagement or frustration and for discovering the hubs of relational energy that fuel innovation, purpose, and intrinsic motivation.

- **Vicarious Reflection:** Thankfully we don't have to learn every lesson first-hand. A close cousin to Anticipatory Reflection, Vicarious Reflection uses other people's real-life experiences or business cases as the focal point. The difference is that when EALs reflect on the experiences of others, they also pay attention to their embodied experience. What do they feel as they put themselves in the shoes of those who lived through it? What can they learn, and what adaptations might they make based on the feedback they receive from their embodied reflection? In addition to informing courses of action, this type of reflection is helpful for leaders who want to develop empathy and emotional intelligence for themselves and their teams.

Each type of embodied reflection is vital in expanding our awareness and engagement. By becoming aware of and reflecting on our embodied experience, we open a world of new possibilities for success.

Transforming Through Embodied Awareness

Abbie's experience on the mountain and leading her team demonstrates that we don't need to be hijacked by our nervous system's well-meaning but clumsy attempts to preserve our safety. With self-awareness, we can recognize the signs of negativity bias and make an intentional shift to overcome it.

The first step is being mindfully aware of and understanding our embodied experience in high-stress situations or even as we anticipate venturing from the safety of our familiar surroundings for a new challenge or opportunity. For me, my heartbeat usually starts to race, signaling real or perceived impending threat, as it did in the start area on that icy racecourse in Palisades Tahoe. Neuroscientist Joseph LeDoux refers to this as a change of body state, or COBS.[4] Your COBS might start with the awareness of feeling your face flush or a sudden shift in your mood or demeanor. Next, you might ask yourself if that irritability is just low blood sugar or if your biology is resisting delving into the unknown.

With practice and repetition, becoming aware of your embodied signals becomes easier, and it becomes more natural to take a breath and slow down the fight-freeze-flight reaction. This pause for embodied awareness is often enough to create a COBS. This intentional shift is another example of cognitive reappraisal. It can make the difference between being engulfed by your reactive, negativity bias and having an embodied agile response.[4] With awareness, we can shift from the mindset that sends us running away from the unfamiliar to one that welcomes fresh perspectives and choices that embrace delightful opportunities. In a mindset of possibility, the sophisticated areas of our brain can think creatively and see novel relationships, ideas, and opportunities that the reptilian brain cannot.

Become Comfortable with Being Uncomfortable

Although embodied awareness is a great place to start, awareness alone doesn't always result in a miraculous COBS. Assessing and understanding the risks with our head may not be enough to convince our heart and gut, let alone the rest of our body, to come along for the ride. Thankfully, we don't need to force ourselves into a different body state or mindset. Another strategy is to accept our discomfort and anxiety and expand our capacity to be comfortable with being uncomfortable.

Organizational psychologist Phillip Mirvis discovered that team members who balanced their fears and misgivings with an appreciation of their years of training and experience were the most effective. He calls this state of mind "anxious confidence." Rather than fight the anxiety, EALs welcome it as a sign of high engagement.[5] They have confidence in their skills, knowledge, and talent—and an appropriate level of anxiety to respond to the inevitable unexpected obstacles. Anxious confidence also is the mindset of improvisers who create entire evenings of theater based on one or two suggestions from the audience. They expect the unexpected and welcome it as a beautiful gift to be enthusiastically accepted. They are confident that, while they don't know how the story will unfold, they can think on their feet and create it in the moment.

Improvisers don't develop their confidence by accident, either. While they don't "rehearse" their performances because there is technically nothing to "re-hear," they do gather regularly to play improv games and improvise with random suggestions (givens). These improvisations help them be more comfortable when co-creating in front of a live audience. EALs do the same. They know they can't formally rehearse for a new role, but they can play out various scenarios or convene other confidence-building "workout" sessions or "training runs."

It was this kind of preparation and Abbie's inspiration that gave me the presence of mind and body at the top of that icy racecourse to make this shift. With my heart pounding and my smartwatch blaring, I took a few deep breaths, and remembered that I had trained in these conditions and that I had the skills and ability to take on this new challenge. It wasn't that my confidence lifted my anxiety. Rather, it partnered with it so I could launch out of the starting gate in a state of high performance—and achieve a 2-second lead for the gold!

Slow Down to Go Fast

In high-stakes games, whether business or ski racing, practicing embodied reflection may seem counterintuitive because it requires us to slow down. The good news is that slowing down can help you go even faster. Engineer and ski racer Mike "Geronimo" Lanier describes how he practices slowing down to go fast racing down the mountain and managing complex projects:

> When you are doing those speed events, like Super G, you have to focus. I'm also a martial artist, and I've learned that when you zone in, time slows down. In ski racing, when you're fully focused on the next gate or the two gates ahead of you, and you know it's only gonna be something like 50 milliseconds between gates but it feels like a good 10 or 15 seconds. I love that feeling. I'm going downhill 60 miles an hour on a turn, and if one of my skis goes out from under

me, I can bring it back in midair because I'm in the present moment, and everything is slowed down. I can feel it.

At work, it's the same thing. I'm at my best when things are on fire, nobody can figure out what to do, and things are moving fast because, to me, everything slows down. I can slow everything down and be in that moment when everyone else is pulling their hair out. But I can see the things that need to happen in real time because I'm kind of just zoned in.

It is not that leaders who embody agility have some special thrill-seeking gene; it is that they recognize that every challenge includes enormous opportunities to stretch, grow, learn, and achieve. Adopting a mindset of continuous learning and adaptation is how EALs remove the obstacles to getting in the game, adapting to all the unexpected and unplanned changes. New learning with each iteration, in turn, fosters new competence, capacity, and confidence that they can draw on for future performance. Plus, new learning inspires additional energy and engagement for even more passion, purpose, and pleasure as they play.

A Framework for Embodied Reflection and Action

The opportunity to transform the barriers I described in Chapter 3 into growth opportunities is too good to leave to chance. You've seen how EALs make this intentional shift in their workplaces and on the mountain. In each instance, they initiate a cycle of embodied reflection that leads to effective action. Their mindset of learning and adaptation rather than planning and controlling sets them apart. The

Embodied Reflection and Action Cycle is a framework that will help you approach each new challenge as a growth opportunity.

This framework will be an excellent resource for you. Once you become familiar with this cycle and practice a few loops yourself, you will find it soon develops into a habit, allowing you to stay in the game and stay in the moment—the only time when effective action is possible.

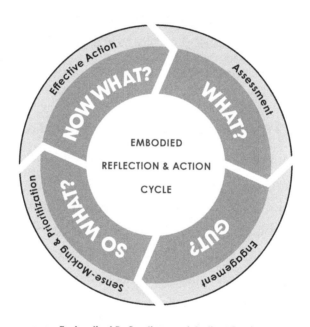

Embodied Reflection and Action Cycle

Embodied reflection will help you seize new opportunities and build on your successes. You can turn challenges into opportunities by first becoming aware of and reflecting on your current reality, including possible barriers. The cycle will serve as the coaching framework while topic-specific reflective questions will guide your progress going forward. I describe each of the Embodied Reflection and Action Cycle stages below so you can become familiar with them.

Take a Breath (or 10)

The best way to slow down and begin your cycle of embodied reflection is to close your eyes (if possible) and take one, or ideally 10, deep breaths: in through your nose, out through your mouth.

With each inhale, draw in energy and bring your awareness to a new area of your body, emotions, and finally, your surroundings. With each exhale, release any tension or blockage you discover.

Notice and embrace your changed body state.

- **What?** *Practicing Embodied Awareness and Assessment*

    This initial stage is the most important and will help ensure that you are responsive rather than reactive to new challenges or opportunities. It invites you to become aware of what is going on with your whole, embodied self and your environment. Your "What?" can be as narrow and immediate as the pain in your left big toe after a stumble or as broad and long-ranging as emerging geopolitical unrest in another country. Depending on its complexity and scope, your "What?" may take seconds or weeks to assess. The important thing is that you pause long enough to do it.

- **Gut?** *Engaging Your Whole Person*

    You may be tempted to skip this stage. But it's important to complete it because it invites you to get in touch with what you are feeling in your heart and gut in response to what is happening. Checking in at this level can bring awareness to responses and feelings that can inform whether your experience is depleting or energizing you. More than a turn of phrase, when you pause to do a "gut check" before a major decision, you are practicing embodied reflection. The gut and brain constantly communicate, connected by "an extensive network of neurons and a highway of chemicals and hormones that constantly provide feedback."[6] A queasy stomach, racing heart, or other body sensations may signal anxiety, anger, frustration, sadness, or despair, helping you know if it is time to regroup or marshal additional resources. Or you may become aware of feeling calm, joyful, excited, optimistic, or inspired. Both kinds of responses include important information. Becoming aware of what you and your colleagues are feeling about what is going on and, if possible, gauging the intensity of your and others' engagement (or lack thereof) is important information to carry into the next cycle stage.

- **So What?** *Making Sense and Prioritizing*

It is one thing to become aware of what is happening and another to make sense of and determine what priority to give your discoveries. You can ask "So What?" on your own, although it can be helpful to invite a few friends or colleagues to join you in many situations. Collaboration often increases clarity about the relevancy and urgency of what is happening and can even determine what is within your sphere of influence. With this clarity, you can more quickly prioritize your options and cycle through the next stage.

- **Now What?** *Making Decisions and Acting*

    Good decisions and actions must be timely and effective. Timeliness is, of course, relative. If you are in immediate physical danger or have an urgent customer issue, timeliness may be counted on a stopwatch. In contrast, a timely response to complex issues, such as a new competitor in your market or a personal health issue, may be tracked on a calendar.

Regardless of the time it takes, EALs know they cannot determine their "Now What?" without slowing down to complete at least one loop through the Embodied Reflection and Action Cycle. EALs approach each iteration as an experiment. With this mindset, they begin the cycle again after completing their first loop, asking a new "What?" For example, they ask what happened because of their experiment and assess what they learned and what is getting their attention now. This is a familiar cycle for countless teams across thousands of organizations that practice Agile frameworks.[7] Each work cycle or "sprint" is bookended with a review of the outcomes and a retrospective on the work process. Leaders and team members apply their insights and lessons learned to the next work cycle, improving their outcomes and capability.

As I have shared, you need not adopt an Agile framework to benefit from some of their best practices. All you need is the intention to slow down enough to discover the reality of the present moment and the desire to learn and adapt through embodied reflection. Give yourself this gift of iterative reflection to clarify your intentions and transform them into effective actions. Timely decisions must, of course, also be effective. The must positively resolve the situation or generate new pathways forward.

COACHING

Transforming Obstacles into Opportunities

This chapter's coaching questions can help you practice embodied reflection and make shifts to transform your obstacles to staying in the game into opportunities for learning and growth.

With your responses to the previous chapters' coaching questions and the four Ps of your game in mind, write your responses to each of these questions. Feel free to pause before moving into each new stage of the cycle.

 Download the *Embodied Reflection and Action Journal* with all of the coaching prompts, as well as additional resources here: https://pamela-meyer.com/staying-in-the-game-resources/ or use the QR code on the left.

What?
 	
Practicing Embodied Awareness and Assessment
	• What is getting my attention at this point?
	
	• What embodied experiences did I notice as I was reading the stories and thinking about my own life?
	
	• When I think about the experiences in which I am most engaged and enjoying the four Ps (play, purpose, passion, and pleasure):
	
	    ◦ What, if any, risks or barriers do I encounter?
	
	    ◦ What, if any, risks or barriers are getting in the way of my getting in, or staying in, the game?
	
	    ◦ Alternatively, what will it cost me NOT to get in or stay in the game?
	
	• What are the rewards of staying in the game?

Gut? *Engaging Your Whole Person*	• What feelings and sensations am I experiencing in response to the risks, barriers, and rewards I have identified? (And have I felt this before? And, if yes, how did I respond, and what did I learn from that experience?) • Which of these embodied responses is getting my attention? • If relevant, what are others feeling, and what is getting their attention in relation to the risks, barriers, and rewards you have collectively identified?
So What? *Making Sense and Prioritizing*	• Which of my insights above are most relevant to my game (purpose, passion, pleasure, and ability to play)? • Which of these potential risks, barriers, and rewards are within my/our span of influence or control? • What are my available resources to respond to them? • Which of these insights, if any, require an immediate response?
Now What? *Making Decisions and Acting*	• If a response is needed, what decisions, actions, or adaptations will have the greatest impact (help me get in and stay in the game, support positive outcomes)? • What obstacles are getting in the way of my success? • How can I or who/what can I engage to help remove these obstacles? • What new habits or practices will help me sustain my progress?

PART II
THE DYNAMICS OF BEING IN THE GAME

With a renewed relationship to your "what" and "why," you have identified potential obstacles and begun clearing them from your path. You are now ready to discover and begin experimenting with your "how." In the chapters ahead, I describe several ways that Embodied Agile Leaders (EALs) find, adapt to, and stay in the game. You will learn more about each of the dynamics that motivate and sustain EALs to bring their best selves to the game. You will also gain a fuller appreciation of the symbiotic relationship between the "what" and "why" of your game and the "how" of being in it as an EAL.

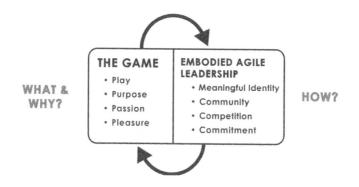

CHAPTER 5

MEANINGFUL IDENTITY

Naming and Claiming Your Core

Dave Clark painted a vivid picture of how his experience of Embodied Agile Leadership shapes his Meaningful Identity and permeates his mindset and work. Though he is now retired, when I first interviewed him by phone, he was sitting at his office desk. He shared, "I have pictures here, and I have photographs of me in my race suit from the NASTAR Nationals in 2013, and I have pictures of me golfing and water skiing, and pictures of me on my kayak. I have a photograph of me standing on a podium at the 2014 NASTAR Nationals, getting a medal. It's part of my identity. It's how I see myself."

> It's how I see myself.
>
> —Dave Clark, 78-year-old multisport athlete and I.T. Project Manager

Dave's description exemplifies a theme that emerges in almost every encounter I have with Embodied Agile Leaders (EALs). I first got to know Dave during weekend races at Wilmot Mountain in Wisconsin. Without fail, he showed up with an infectious, positive, and enthusiastic mindset and attitude.

Meaningful Identity, or the meaningful ways we see ourselves and show up in the world is ingrained in our game, and the game is ingrained in our identity. We generate meaning and purpose through this symbiotic relationship. EALs share a keen awareness of what gives their life meaning, and that meaning is at the core of their identity.

Explorations of identity and how we develop it has a long, rich, and lively history that continues to evolve in psychology, sociology, cultural and anthropological studies, and beyond.[1] My aim in this chapter is not to trek into this broader territory but, at the same time, not to leave out the other significant dimensions of identity that inform EALs' embodied experience of the four Ps of the game. These include the intersections of our cultural, racial, ethnic, age, ability, neurodiversity, and sexual and gender identity. These dimensions become especially significant as EALs find and co-create Community, as you will learn in Chapter 6. The Meaningful Identity in focus in this chapter centers on how we come to know ourselves specifically in relation to the game and how our engagement in the game, in turn, helps us embrace and live into that Meaningful Identity.

Becoming an Embodied Agile Leader

Sometimes it takes hearing how others see you before you can claim it for yourself.

According to developmental psychologist Robert Kegan *"Human being is meaning-making."*[2] It is not separate from our other activities but central to them. I was reminded of the dynamic nature of meaning-making as I experimented with various fitness strategies to prepare for an upcoming ski season. While CrossFit didn't end up being the right approach for me, I loved the camaraderie I found there and how seriously the coaches took all of us, no matter our age or fitness level. It may seem like such a simple thing, but it made a huge difference for me that each session started with the coach gathering us up from our various stretching and warm-up routines by shouting, *"Listen up, athletes!"*

The first time the coach called out for the athletes to gather around to review the session's workout, I looked around the gym to see if he was talking to another group, one that couldn't possibly include me. While I had maintained a fitness routine for much of my life, I certainly didn't think of myself as an *athlete*. Athletes are young, ultra-fit, and highly competitive, characteristics I wouldn't have used to describe myself. I soon realized that this coach was giving us all a gift—an opportunity to own and live into an identity that we might not yet be claiming. It took someone else taking me seriously before I could start to take myself seriously.

The *meaningfulness* of identity is dynamic and evolves over time. Once you begin the journey, the impact is tangible and significant. Like Dave and the many other EALs I work and train with, I soon discovered that when I began to name and claim my identities, my engagement in Community (Chapter 5), Competition (Chapter 6), and Commitment (Chapter 7) only grew.

Dress for Success

Sometimes Meaningful Identity develops from the outside in before we can own it from the inside out. For me, this has sometimes meant taking myself seriously enough to aspire to a new emerging identity. For example, as I became known as an expert in business agility, taking myself seriously meant pursuing a doctorate in midlife. As a novice ski racer, it meant training with a coach, attending race camps and clinics, and eventually ponying up the cash (and confidence) to buy a race suit. These investments were not just financial but a signal to myself and others that I was serious.

Dressing for success in ski racing is literal. It means shimmying into a skintight suit designed for optimal aerodynamics. I admit that I wasn't eager to step out of my comfort zone (and out of my comfy snow pants) and step (actually, squeeze) into my new purple suit. And yet, for me, claiming my Meaningful Identity as a competitive racer meant setting my ego aside and doing just that.

Wearing my suit on race days taught me valuable lessons about Meaningful Identify. First, self-consciousness evaporates when you are with others with shared four Ps. Second, while it is hard to say how much of a difference the suits make in our race times on any given day, it greatly impacts how we see ourselves and our sense of belonging. Even though I had been to a few local races wearing my bib over my ski jacket and snow pants, no one seemed to "see" me until I wore a race suit. Once in the suit, others saw a committed athlete, and I began to receive helpful tips from fellow racers. In turn, this motivated me to train more seriously and seek more coaching, which increased the number of times I made it onto the podium, not to mention how much more fun I had! Naming and claiming my Meaningful Identity soon became a positive self-fulfilling prophecy.

My friend, coach, and consultant Cate Creede shared her version of dressing for success some years ago. She was becoming increasingly uncomfortable with the impact of years of smoking and the extra pounds she had put on from a more sedentary lifestyle. One day, she decided to quit and "start living like someone who doesn't smoke." Each day, even several times a day, she asked herself, "What choice would someone who doesn't smoke make right now?" or "How would someone who doesn't smoke enjoy their weekend?" Before long, she was running several miles a day and, to date, has logged thousands of miles cycling around the world. My friend's approach, of course, is not for everyone. However, sometimes starting to live into the Meaningful Identity you aspire to is enough to set a positive generative cycle in motion. You feel better and are more engaged in your newly claimed Meaningful Identity, which spurs more Commitment.

Taking Your Meaningful Identity Seriously

> The only difference between
> a creative person and a non-creative
> person is that a creative person
> takes his or her ideas seriously.
>
> —**Mary Zimmerman, Tony Award Winning Theater Director**

Naming and claiming your Meaningful Identity is motivating and clarifying. Dorian "Doc" Paskowitz, who died at 93, identified as "a surfer first, Jew second, doctor third."[3] When Paskowitz discovered that his Meaningful Identity was "surfer first," he moved to California with his wife and seven kids and started a surfing school. He didn't wait for permission from some external authority or for someone to tell him he was good enough, financially stable enough, or otherwise "ready." Through his passion for surfing, he found his purpose, which propelled him through a lifetime of sharing the pleasure and play of the game with countless others.

You certainly don't need to discover Meaningful Identity through sports. Still, there is a common theme in athletes' experiences that can help all of us discover, appreciate, and embrace our energizing core. Researcher Gad Yair found that identity was a critical motivator for runners beyond the racecourse.[4] He found that the desire to remain competitive well beyond their peak years can set off a virtuous cycle with the desire to maintain an identity as a "capable person" over the long haul. When Meaningful Identity grows out of active engagement, we are more likely to continue to seek out opportunities to participate and sustain Commitment.

> **When Meaningful Identity grows out of active engagement, we are more likely to continue to seek out opportunities to participate and sustain Commitment.**

Seriously, But Not Too Seriously

Whether shimmying into a race suit, wet suit, or any other suit, raising your hand for the stretch assignment, pursuing a new learning experience, or jumping into any other activity that reflects your seriousness about playing the game, we can all start to take ourselves a little *too* seriously. It helps to remember that our identities are dynamic; they will always be in flux as we participate in and adapt to changes in our relationships, teams, organizations, and countless others outside our control.

Over the several years span of my research, I witnessed EALs as they moved through many of these shifts, including professional role shifts, retirements, injury, illness, and other life changes, and even gender identification. Adapting to these shifts and the new discoveries we make about ourselves takes courage, humility, and a good dose of humor. When we lose our sense of humor and ability to play with and within our Meaningful Identity, we risk becoming derailed by setbacks, large and small. Without a bit of levity, how can you possibly step into your race suit on game day?

Playspace for Meaningful Identity

It was during my early leadership agility research[5,6] that I discovered the crucial space we co-create as we learn and experiment. I came to call this space "playspace" because it enables people to step out of their comfort zone, take risks, discover, and experiment with new capabilities and versions of themselves. We cannot discover and experiment without a mindset and space for this kind of play. Don't be fooled by your learned associations with the word "play," which implies frivolity. Play is even more important in complex and high-stakes life and work contexts because success requires room and support to continue to explore and experiment. Play occurs in laboratories, conference rooms, lunchrooms, shop floors, and other onsite and virtual spaces where we gather to work and co-create.

Identifying Meaningful Identity

If you had asked me earlier in my life, when I was working as a theater director and producer, to describe my Meaningful Identity, I would have a very different answer than I do today. Because identity is not static, how you know yourself in the world changes, as does how you are known in the world. Throughout your life and career, you will accumulate and cycle through roles as diverse as child, partner, parent, counselor, mediator, manager, caregiver, coach, director, advocate, cheerleader, guide, servant, and teacher, to name just a few possibilities. And you will often play many of those roles simultaneously. This means we do not so much possess an "identity" as participate in the continuous practice of *identifying*.

Turns out that a lot of us are actively identifying. The most recent US Department of Labor study found that baby boomers held an average of 12.4 jobs between 18 and 54, with nearly half being held from ages 18–24.[7] Job-hopping is even more popular with millennials. Global employment mobility and volatility have only increased in response to COVID-19.

In addition to changes in your role, work, job, or career focus that can affect your Meaningful Identity, other planned and unplanned disruptions are common. Life changes, both happy and sad, such as marriage, divorce, death, and children, can shake you to your core. An illness or injury can rattle your sense of yourself as a capable person and trigger a crisis in confidence. Unplanned job loss or retirement can also disrupt your sense of identity and what is meaningful within it. In the best scenarios, with support and in Community, you will move through and construct a renewed and reenergized sense of yourself in the world that aligns with your current capabilities and, perhaps, a new or transformed game. Those who take advantage of the new territory for reflection and reorientation often find the discomfort and uncertainty of such uncharted territory are also the most fertile ground for new possibilities, passions, and capabilities to emerge.

Meeting the Moment with Your Meaningful Identity

New and often expanded possibilities are the space Catherine Marienau, Professor Emerita at DePaul University, and her colleague entrepreneur Gail Zelitzky, explore through hundreds of conversations with women who are thriving into their 70s, 80s, 90s, and even 100s on their podcast, WomenOver70—Aging Reimagined.[8] These women include civil rights and business leaders, activists, artists, educators, and entrepreneurs. Catherine shared, "In many cases, core aspects of these women's identity or what they value endure as they cycle through multiple, multifaceted roles. Their sense of identity might be driven by deeply held beliefs, early formative experiences, or the context they grew up in or in which they began their work lives." For many EALs, whose experiences I describe below, core values continue to guide them, even as their Meaningful Identity shifts to meet the moment.

The lessons from those adapting to the current moment to stay in the game are instructive and inspiring. Fortunately, you don't have to log 70+ years to develop the ability to continuously rediscover, reinvent, and adapt your Meaningful Identity to meet *your* moment. This secret is also shared by CEOs, activists, entrepreneurs, and many others who know that sometimes when the game changes, so too does how they participate in the game—and maybe even what costume they wear to it! You will discover what meeting the moment with (and through) Meaningful Identity looks like for three impactful EALs in the stories that follow.

Meeting the Moment as a Disrupter

A long-distance runner who learned the "rules of the game" at Harvard and MIT,[9] John Legere was tapped in 2012 to take on the role of CEO for T-Mobile and elevate the company in the highly competitive game of wireless telecom. Leading the rebranded "un-carrier," John and T-Mobile disrupted the telecom industry by bucking norms in a relentless pursuit of growth driven by customer value. It wasn't long before John transformed his outward appearance, trading his buttoned-up finance guy suits (first at AT&T and then Asia Global Crossing) for magenta-logoed tracksuits. He not only embraced a new Meaningful Identity to meet the moment, but he also co-created the moment.[10] The transformation, however, wasn't immediate. Much more than just a new marketing tagline, the strategies and tactics were truly disruptive and included ripping up the customer-unfriendly contracts of limited data plans. Meaningful Identity evolves, often incrementally. John shared, "If you saw the announcement video that was sent to all T-Mobile employees announcing me as CEO, I was in a proper suit, my hair was slicked back, and my speech was, well, boring."[11]

John understood that his outward appearance needed to reflect his current Meaningful Identity and be as dynamic as the company and industry he was leading. "The change at T-Mobile needed to start with me," he said. "I knew I needed to go all the way in order to change the culture to something that reflected who we were, or would be, as a company.... I grew out my hair, swapped out the suit and tie for a leather jacket and a magenta T-shirt, and threw away the filter."[12]

In addition to leading with a disruptive strategy and tactics, John led with learning and agility and invested in developing leaders across the United States to do the same. During this time, I collaborated with his team of talent development professionals, led by Melissa Davis and Melissa Lanier Preston, on an innovative leadership development program based on my book *The Agility Shift*.[13] This investment was especially critical in the high-growth years leading up to the Sprint merger. Leaders across the organization needed to develop their agility capability to live into the promise of the un-carrier branding.[14] This approach paid off with an unprecedented 27 straight quarters of growth in which the company added more than one million new subscribers per quarter, nearly quadrupling subscribers through to the long-cultivated Sprint merger in 2020.[15] This period required both the endurance and agile mindset of a long-distance runner, for which

John was prepared through his years in college as a competitive runner, as well as by his years running other businesses. Even if running isn't your game, leading with a dynamic, Meaningful Identity requires an athlete's discipline, stamina, and agility.

Meeting the Moment as a Learning Leader

This same discipline, stamina, and agility were essential for Desiree Adaway when she took a risk and left her demanding job as Senior Director of Volunteer Mobilization at Habitat for Humanity. Her departure wasn't because she wasn't making a difference or impacting the important work of "bringing people together to build homes, communities, and hope."[16] She was. For Desiree, meeting the moment meant expanding her Meaningful Identity and impact by transferring the skills, knowledge, and talent she had developed over years of leading international teams in global nonprofits and Fortune 500 companies. It was time to meet *her* moment. I was lucky to connect with Desiree at this exciting time when she was on the brink of yet another role shift and evolution of her Meaningful Identity. She knew it was time to engage her experience and wisdom gathered through the years to start The Adaway Group, a Black woman–owned consulting firm that brings together multiracial teams to work on equity, inclusion, and social justice projects.[17]

This shift enabled Desiree to align her passion and purpose more deeply and to share her wisdom, experience, and lessons learned earlier in her career. This insight, combined with her rigorous study of social movements and continuous learning is one of the many reasons Desiree has made such an impact in creating space for others to learn and transform. By taking the lead in sharing her experience, she helps create what she refers to as a "brave space" for others to do the same. This space balances challenge and support and can foster deep reflection and courageous conversations in which others can also discover their Meaningful Identity. Desiree shared one particularly hard-won lesson she learned in one of her first roles leading camps for kids from public housing. She discovered how her Commitment to her work at the time had led her to return to work to lead a staff training session just two days after giving birth to her second child.

> We tell stories about how important we are and how we're irreplaceable. And the reality is that that training could have happened without me, and I would never, ever, ever get those days back with my kids. It's one of my biggest regrets. I look back, and I'm like, "That's not what being a leader was." Because the reality is, somebody should have told me to go sit down. Our boss at the time should've said, "You should not be here working." But they didn't. They allowed me to work. I look back now, and I'm like, "Oh, that's the patriarchy." There was this expectation. I think this is not only as a woman but also as a Black woman, this expectation that I have to show up, even when it's to my detriment. But I have to show up in certain ways to navigate society, or I lose opportunities.

Many women, particularly women of color whom I have interviewed and work with, shared similar experiences of how their sense of themselves had become negatively entwined with others' perceptions and expectations and was developed within a system that prioritized maintaining its current power structures over their well-being and growth. It is an identity but not one that is sustainable or ultimately meaningful. Desiree took this wisdom into the many leadership roles that followed. By learning to step back, she shared that she could provide others with opportunities to step up to career-shaping roles. The evolutionary nature of Meaningful Identity informs the journey of all EALs. Desiree met the moment, and the moment met her.

In response to the killing of George Floyd in May 2020, corporations and nonprofits across the United States and beyond began to look in the mirror with a greater willingness and Commitment to make meaningful change than ever before. Desiree and her team at The Adaway Group were experienced and ready to respond. "People hire me to help them say things that should have been said years ago," she shared. They fielded hundreds of calls from organizations across sectors and continue to lead countless workshops and consulting engagements with those who are ready to do the hard work needed to transform their workplaces into more equitable, diverse, and inclusive environments where everyone can thrive.

Meeting the Moment as an Agile Leader

Throughout his career, James Hlavenka, Esq., has centered his Meaningful Identity around his core values and purpose: to help serve others, whom he knows are the ultimate beneficiaries of his efforts. Jim's identity as a respected pharmaceutical industry attorney was developed over the years and is deeply rooted in his humanistic values of integrity and the importance of collaboration. His career path was motivated by the devasting impact his family experienced after a medication that a family member had taken for two decades to manage his health suddenly stopped working. Overnight, the stability of Jim's family was upended, followed by cascading turmoil. In pursuit of answers and motivated to ensure other families did not suffer this kind of impact, Jim combined a science-driven education with a J.D. in health law.

Like most sectors, the US healthcare environment continues to evolve rapidly. It is more volatile, uncertain, complex, and ambiguous than ever. Patients and physicians surged to telehealth and related health technologies during the pandemic; hospitals continue to integrate to create large and intricate healthcare systems and operate in a climate of regulatory and legislative uncertainty, to name a few dynamics. Jim and his leadership colleagues knew that to compete and lead in this environment, they needed to reimagine how they worked to remain responsive and relevant to these ever-changing conditions and related needs. For instance, the classic pharmaceutical industry model of relying solely on in-person sales representatives no longer equals success in a virtual and tech-forward healthcare world; business and marketing strategies needed to rapidly evolve to meet physicians and patients at home outside the doctor's office.

In this landscape, Jim was offered an opportunity to deepen his impact at UCB (a global biopharmaceutical company) by leaving the legal department and taking on the role of Head of Agility Enablement within UCB's US Neurology division. The transition from Legal Counselor to Agility Enabler was not without its risks, personally and professionally. This opportunity would mean a significant shift for Jim as he would be transitioning away from the role he was professionally trained in and had worked for over a decade. In addition, it would mean taking on an entirely new role after almost six years of serving as senior counsel in the same division.

With an agile mindset, Jim prioritized learning and adapting over control. He knew that the fears, uncertainty, and perceived risks signaled that he was entering new territories for opportunity and growth. Rather than remain in his comfort zone, Jim chose to lean outside of his professional training to do what both scared and energized him most—pursue an opportunity to do something different in a risk-averse industry. In seizing the opportunity, Jim weighed the hoped-for reward of positively benefiting people and patients on a national scale, against the risk of uncertainty. There was no guarantee that he could translate the success he found in law within the commercial business context. As an EAL, Jim knew that leading a game-changing transformation in his organization and possibly his industry at large was also an opportunity to stay relevant to the passion, purpose, and values at the core of his Meaningful Identity.

Much like Jim's personal transformation, organizational Agile transformations are rarely comfortable. The shift to adopting agile methodologies outside of a software environment, while a growing trend today, is still novel in pharma and particularly outside of R&D. Leading an agile transformation in a cross-functional business group demanded that Jim shift his way of thinking and working while simultaneously helping others to embrace doing the same as well. He described what this shift from a Meaningful Identify as an expert with a command and control-driven approach to one of peer-based collaboration and co-creation looked and felt like.

> This [agile] model says, yes, raise your hand, provide ideas; you're a valued team member. You're not here to give your one answer to this one question. You don't need permission to provide value "outside your swim lane." This was an entirely new way of conducting business, and many were

hesitant to embrace it. Over time, with psychological safety and permission to fail, we're seeing these bright eyes saying, "we have something better here. We would never have thought we could do this, but we are doing it, and we are creating better output as a result of collective participation."

With Jim's leadership and modeling, the shift to cross-functional collaboration allowed all Agile team members to embrace discomfort and live more deeply into their Meaningful Identities while achieving remarkable results.

Claiming Your Meaningful Identity for a Dynamic Future

Each of these examples, and likely your own experience, reinforce that naming and claiming your Meaningful Identify is not a one-and-done endeavor. You will hear more about each of the three leaders' practice of Embodied Agile Leadership and their impact later in the book.

Like so many aspects of life and learning, the best way to begin the process of identifying your Meaningful Identity is to *begin the process*. Most EALs are the first to admit that the discovery and development of their Meaningful Identity is rarely smooth sailing. No compelling adventure story ever is! No matter how many cookbooks you read, you must get in the kitchen and make a mess, burn a few pots, and experience triumphs and disasters to learn the nuances of a particular recipe and even cooking in general. All EALs know that the goal is not some perfect end state but an engaged, dynamic mindset of continuous learning and adaptation (Chapter 7). EALs expect not only to respond to new experiences and discoveries but also to be transformed by them through each iteration. As you continue these cycles of learning and adapting you will also find yourself not only identifying your meaning, but meaning with your identity.

COACHING

Discovering Your Meaningful Identity

Using the Embodied Reflection and Action Cycle prompt questions for this chapter, begin the next iteration of reflection to discover more about your Meaningful Identity.

 Download the *Embodied Reflection and Action Journal* with all of the coaching prompts, as well as additional resources here: https://pamela-meyer.com/staying-in-the-game-resources/ or use the QR code on the left.

What? *Practicing Embodied Awareness and Assessment*	• What am I learning in response to my reading, reflections, and actions so far? • With the four Ps of your Game from Chapter 1 in mind, reflect on words that you use today to describe your Meaningful Identity. Be bold and aspirational. • What do you feel like as you embody your Meaningful Identity? You might start by using this simple sentence starter (remember, you are not looking for a final description, just today's description): I am a.... • *Example: "I am a..." resilient, engaged athlete, author, and educator.* • With the embodied experience of your Meaningful Identity freshly engaged, reflect on what experiences, interactions, and activities contribute to your identity.
Gut? *Engaging Your Whole Person*	• Close your eyes momentarily and envision yourself fully embodying your Meaningful Identity. Allow yourself to experience your Meaningful Identity fully. Don't rush. Once you have spent time here, reflect on how you feel. Depending on where you are, you might even experiment with moving your body in a way that expresses or amplifies your experience. Alternatively, consider drawing or painting an image expressing your lived experience. These embodied reflections may be enough for you to move into the next stage of the cycle. Remember that you can revisit these reflections over time, so I encourage you to take a few more minutes to describe your embodied experience, noting as many dimensions of your head, heart, and gut as possible.
So What? *Making Sense and Prioritizing*	• To your description above, add any reflections on ways it is important for you to be known by your family, professional colleagues, and other Communities to which you belong. • If you named several aspects of your Meaningful Identity, could you prioritize those most important to you or aligned with your values today? Remember Dorian Paskowitz, who prioritized being a "surfer first..." • If time or resources are constrained, which aspects of your identity do you want to prioritize?

Now What? *Making Decisions and Acting*	• How do you or might you "dress for success" to live into your EAL identity? • Are any additional resources worth investing in (e.g., training, coaching, technology, equipment) to help you live into your identity? • Are there any obstacles getting in the way of you living your Meaningful Identity? How might you remove them? • With these insights in mind, what actions can you take or activities do you want to prioritize, invest in, or make a habit of that will reinforce and energize your experience of Meaningful Identity?

CHAPTER 6

COMMUNITY

Tapping the Power of People

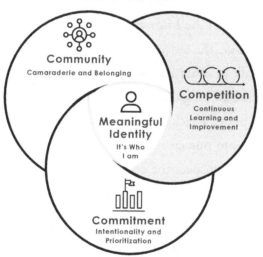

As I pull into our small Wisconsin ski area, the lifts have not yet begun turning. The temperature on my car thermometer is reading –7° Fahrenheit, making it closer to –20° with the windchill. I wave to my fellow club racers, pulling into frozen spaces, unloading their gear, and making the icy trek to the base lodge.

After several years, I have come to cherish this pre-race ritual. When I enter the lodge, almost without fail, my racing friend Karl and his friends, Toshio and Max, have already arrived and staked out their table. Karl Landl was proudly wearing bib #54 when I first met him, which coincidently announced the number of years he had been racing. Originally from Austria, he came to the United States as a young man setting out on what he thought was, at most, a few-year adventure. Now some six decades later, with a thriving life outside of Chicago, he has retired from his career as a precision machinist.

His long-time racing friends include Toshio Ogino, an alternate for the Japanese Alpine Ski Team for the 1960 Winter Olympics, and Max Ferstl, a youngster still in his 70s who immigrated to the United States as a young man from Bavaria. Surprisingly, Max didn't learn to ski until he arrived in the Midwest.

On race days, the warm hellos and how-ya-beens mix with playful trash talk as other racers continue to arrive and claim their territories in the base lodge. We organize our gloves, goggles, helmets, race bibs, and boots; check in with the volunteer race director; and finally shimmy into our race suits before heading out to take a few warm-up runs and inspect the course before we line up at the start for the first race of the day.

The Essence of Community

The camaraderie we share on these race days and training sessions is the essence of Community, the magnetic force that attracts us to be in the game. It holds us together through the ups and downs of the season and helps us stay motivated in the months before the next one. This same force draws Embodied Agile Leaders (EALs) to dynamic organizations and motivates them to stay and bring their best performance.

Community is the strongest driver of participation and engagement for many EALs. It is complemented by the two other motivating dynamics of Competition and Commitment that you will learn more about in Chapters 7 and 8. All three interact to construct and sustain the Meaningful Identities of EALs. It is no coincidence that these dynamics share the same Latin root, "com," which means "together."

Each EAL may value or be motivated by a different dynamic depending on their current situation and life circumstances. For example, on an overcast, slushy race day, when I haven't slept well the night before, I might find that being part of the Community is more persuasive to get me out of my cozy bed than my excitement about the Competition. For many of us, Community keeps us coming back year after year, through our good days and bad and helps us maintain our Meaningful Identity.

Amanda Keen has been racing with her family since she was a teenager. Now, as a young entrepreneur, she values the experience of Community more than ever.

> Community is so ingrained, and it's intertwined so that at a certain point, it's part of your identity of being a ski racer. It means everything. The [Community] pushes you. It drives you to do what you love because other people are out there enjoying it, too. For example, someone will volunteer to take our coats down when it gets really cold out. We all know that if you're standing out there without a coat on, you need some help. We're not just competitors, we're also a community. We take care of each other.

While community can define a place or a group of people who share specific characteristics or beliefs, the *experience* of Community (capital C), as Amanda describes, is created by participation and co-creation. Community and the camaraderie found there is one of the most compelling aspects of EALs' desire to return week after week, year after year, in all conditions and through serious setbacks. Because of its importance in motivating EALs to be in the game and perform at their best, I wanted to better understand how these racers and other EALs in business co-create a meaningful experience of Community.

These Community-building insights are critical to sustaining organizational success. Top talent is always at a premium, and leaders need to know how to create environments where talent wants to be and grow. EALs have taught me how important it is to show up for, participate in, and co-create Community in which everyone can thrive.

Show Up

A great place to start learning those secrets is with Karl, Toshio, Max, and their fellow competitors who have been showing up for years. Together they have traveled to races across the Midwest and formed friendships between their families and with other club members. When Karl's wife could no longer come to cheer him on at our local races because of health issues, Max's wife would sometimes step in to care for her on race days so Karl could continue participating. If one of the three is absent on race day, they are missed.

Being missed, it turns out, is one of the hallmarks of Community. My colleague Catherine Marienau and I, at DePaul University's Center to Advance Education for Adults, conducted a series of collaborative inquiries on the nature of Community. We were interested in how people found, co-created, and sustained them. Along the way, we discovered that the best indicator of whether a person was experiencing Community was if they felt that "people miss me when I'm not there." Karl and many other EALs are missed when absent because they participate and help co-create the Community for all to enjoy.

Creating Space for Belonging

Few people understand the value of creating environments of acceptance and belonging in business more than Chris Mikulski, the Head of H.R. Americas for H&M Clothing. He has spent his entire work life in retail and shared that "some of the best times in my career were working in a store because of the diverse community you become a part of." When I asked Chris to tell me more about the value of creating such spaces in the rapidly changing and highly competitive fashion business, he shared,

> [Community] gets you through the challenges and the hard times. And it impacts our ability to be competitive because we inspire each other to do better. We inspire each other to show up. If there's a connection at the other end of your decision, I think you're more likely to make that decision with that connection in mind. So whether it's your favorite person who is closing the store tonight or somebody who you've built a bond with is working…you will be more inclined to make a decision that supports their success and to persevere past doubts or obstacles that we sometimes set for ourselves.

At times when all companies are scrambling to fill jobs with talented, engaged people at all levels of the organization, H&M has leaned into its "Be Yourself & More"[1] recruiting and career development initiatives, which are more relevant than ever. Seventy-six percent of job seekers and employees reported that a diverse workforce is an important factor when evaluating companies and job offers.[2] Companies that truly value diversity don't just stop at the head count; they ensure the heads *count*. Chris described how important this is to him personally and what it means well beyond "words on paper."

> I think naturally, as humans, we seek a sense of belonging in everything we do, even if it's subconsciously. And I think [H&M] works really hard to build that for people. And even myself, being a proud gay man, being so accepted for that here is never questioned. I never have to have two different versions of myself. Even as a leader, that has unlocked my potential to a magnitude I could not have imagined. So that's also why I believe so much in this sense of community, sense of belonging, and safety in those things. Because I've experienced it, and now I can use my platform to create that experience for others, whatever their unique self is.

EALs, such as Chris, understand that fostering Community requires consistent attention and participation. The business impact is significant because when people experience a true sense of belonging in which their Meaningful Identities are seen and valued, they tend to want to stick around. However, the dynamic of Community doesn't happen by chance, as Chris emphasized.

It takes work and an ongoing commitment to that ideal because I think it's easy to look at the world around you and sometimes feel out of lockstep with it. We feel very proud to be these pioneers. I think that's why people want to stay. I've met many people who have been with H&M 10, 15, 20, even 30 years, and then go outside the United States, and it's 30 or 40 years with H&M. It's because they're celebrated as themselves and they feel like they can really contribute authentically. And that's an amazing feeling.

Commitment to creating space for belonging by EALs like Chris at companies like H&M and across industries is critical as the workforce diversifies. The US Department of Labor predicts that by 2024, less than 60% of the workforce will consist of individuals identified as "White, non-Hispanic." Additionally, Latinx individuals are anticipated to comprise almost 20% of the labor force.[3]

Participate

While being missed may seem like a simple indicator of belonging to a Community, the co-creation of it is not so simple. To be missed means that you show up consistently enough to be known and that your presence and contribution are valued. In other words, you are in it not just for yourself but also for the success of others. If we don't co-create Community, it doesn't exist for any of us.

Participating is relational, not simply transactional. No one exemplifies this more than retired I.T. Project Manager Dave Clark, whom you met in Chapter 4. Dave showed up in the finish area to cheer on fellow racers even when his doctors had forbidden him to compete during his cancer treatments. Continuing to participate in Community helped Dave maintain his positive mindset and Meaningful Identity as a healthy, active person through some of the most challenging stretches of his treatment. When his doctors finally gave him the green light to join us back in the gates, we all cheered extra loudly for him.

Co-creating this experience of Community is, for many, a shared effort. For example, my wife is now dubbed the "head cheerleader" because she is a regular in the finish area, distributing cowbells, cheering everyone on, and, before our ski association splurged on an electronic scoreboard, standing at the sandwich boards with a marker in hand, writing each racer's time on the board as they crossed the finish line. Other non-racing friends and family organize the weekly raffle, bring food, and host parking lot barbeques. The point is not so much *what* anyone does but *that we are there* to co-create an experience in which everyone feels included and welcomed.

Leading with participation can look many ways. In your organization, it might be letting people know you missed them when they were out on vacation or cheering on their achievements, awards, or community service—all equivalent to ringing a cowbell in the finish area. And just as important are those who offer to jump in and share the load during crunch times, be as an ally, mentor, or champion, or even to fold that jumble of sweaters on the sale table. It all counts, and it all makes a difference.

Co-Create

Karl was one of the first racers to welcome my wife and me at my first few club races. And if Carol was not with me, without fail, he asked about her by name. If you are used to being an insider, this kind of exchange may be a taken-for-granted pleasantry. As someone who does not take the experience of being included for granted, it made a huge difference in my experience of belonging in the Community.

Building environments that foster belonging are at the heart of diversity, equity, and inclusion efforts across business and social institutions. Such environments do not happen without intention, in a company, or on the race hill.

Practice Radical Hospitality

I was first introduced to the term "radical hospitality" when interviewing an EAL whose playing field is the stage and screen rather than the mountain. Award-winning playwright and Tony-nominated actress and educator Anna Deavere Smith shared that radical hospitality, or the experience of being exuberantly welcomed and included, is needed if we are to bring our best performance.[4] Originating from the Rule of St. Benedict as an edict to welcome the stranger,[5] this practice seems especially radical and needed in polarized climates.

Affinity groups can play that role in the workplace and other environments that want to foster an experience of belonging. The need for such radical hospitality initiatives heightens in spaces that have historically been dominated by one group, as is the case in many industries. Participating in activities and spaces where you don't see anyone who looks like you or shares your life experience (which is often true for people of color, LGBTQ+ people, people with disabilities, and others in predominantly White, straight, able-bodied arenas, such as skiing) amplifies the value of radical hospitality even more.

An excellent place to learn more lessons in creating space for belonging is the ski industry in general and ski racing, in particular. According to a 2021–2022 National Ski Areas Association report, people of color made up only 11% of ski area visits, although they account for almost 40% of the US population.[6,7] The National Brotherhood of Skiers (NBS), an association of now 50 ski clubs, was founded in 1973, a time when it was even rarer to see a person of color on the slopes and rarer yet for people of color to feel welcome and actively included.[8] Miles Maxey, now retired from his career as an engineer at General Motors, and an early NBS member, shared how important the experience of radical hospitality and Community were to his engagement in the sport.

> You felt isolated. NBS started as a group, particularly for African Americans. Three guys who were at university in the 50s wanted to go skiing, but it just wasn't open to them. The networks didn't work, so they started the club. It's a dynamic group of people who are active and willing to go and try to get outside their bubble and find out the world's a lot more fun and more inviting than what it seems. Particularly our experience of skiing and being all over. Our friends have always been really positive. We've got friends of all nationalities pretty much all over the world.

NBS has created a thriving Community that has inspired many people who might not otherwise have had access or felt welcome to participate in snow sports. Their Embodied Agile Leadership reminds us that it's not enough to open the door to participation. When people venture into the unknown, they need to feel welcomed, represented, included, and valued. Leading with radical hospitality means leading with an attitude of appreciation and inquiry. Chris, at H&M, shared that this means:

> If you have blue hair, we want to know what color blue because we love it. If you choose to express yourself through artistic creations and tattoos on your skin, we love that. Whatever brings you joy, I think we seek to intersect with that, not to challenge it or go against it. We want to learn from each person. And I think that's really the celebration of the multidimensional beings that we all are.

For some, embracing different ways of thinking and being in the world is truly radical and uncomfortable. Leading with curiosity rather than judgment is a powerful way to foster Community and inspires others to do the same. What does "welcoming the stranger," as St. Benedict counseled, look like in your Community? How can you ensure that newcomers feel included and valued? Often, it takes just a few words and actions to let someone know you are glad they are here and that you miss them when they are not.

What does "welcoming the stranger" look like in your Community? How can you ensure that newcomers feel included and valued?

Actively valuing each other's presence and participation in Community directly inspires everyone to stay in the game. My friend Karl uses his past experiences of being missed combined with a bit of FOMO (fear of missing out) to get him out to the race hill on days he might be tempted to stay home and skip braving the elements. He shared, "Some days I think, 'Oh, I don't want to go today. The weather is bad, the conditions won't be good.' But then I'll hear, 'Where were you? The skiing was great! We had so much fun!'"

Leading with the New Science of Connectedness

At this point, you may be thinking of your own experiences of Community. You likely also have experienced the joy of being included and the heartache of being excluded. If so, you already know the power of people to elevate or diminish your experience. Scientists confirm the power of connectedness with some fascinating research.

From the earliest sociologic studies[9] to the latest neuroscience,[10] research supports the relational power of people to improve our mental health, happiness, purpose in life, and even financial stability. If these links between connectedness and well-being don't get your attention, the staggering 31% increase in US suicide rates between 2000 and 2020[11] might. Behavioral scientist Dr. Clay Routledge characterized this alarming trend as a "crisis of meaning."[12] If meaning is largely made with and through other people, then the value of Community in fostering overall well-being and livelihood is no surprise. That is just the beginning of the benefits of finding, co-creating, and sustaining your experience of Community. At the risk of sounding like a late-night infomercial pitchwoman, "But wait, there's more!"

Longer Telomeres for Everyone

I first learned about telomeres on yet another chairlift ride in Winter Park, Colorado, with a volunteer guide for the Ski Meisters, "an organization of exceptionally active adults, 55 years and older, who have joined together for the joy of downhill skiing with like-minded individuals."[13] Wearing the signature bright red, yellow, and black jacket of this group, the guide shared how the Ski Meisters is not only a fun way for older skiers to stay in the game but also how such involvement in Community likely improved overall longevity of the participants by increasing the length of their telomeres.

What exactly are telomeres, and how can they affect aging? Strands of repetitive DNA sequences at the ends of our chromosomes, telomeres tend to shorten as we age. This is a problem because telomeres play a critical role in maintaining the ability of healthy cells to fight a wide range of diseases.[14] Based on the scientific view that aging is partly a result of damage to the DNA of our cells over time, longevity researchers believe that this process can be slowed, if not reversed, through social engagement.

Studies increasingly point to the power of positive social engagement on the length of our telomeres, while the reverse is also true. Isolation, or negative engagement, correlates with shortened telomeres.[15,16] While more research needs to be done, the implications of the power of people to impact our overall well-being bolster the case for finding, co-creating, and participating in positive Communities. For those interested in being in the game and playing it as long as possible, active participation in Community, including professional, recreational, and civic, may be your best prescription.

Safety (and Confidence) in Numbers

Still racing at age 77, Barb McCabe was not alone in sharing how the camaraderie of Community that she experiences on race day helps her to not just stay in the game but to stay competitive. She describes her experience racing at the NASTAR nationals:

> Well, it was great. I mean, some total stranger next to me helped me put on my bib. And, you know, he also offered me a little scraper for my goggles. Everybody was just so friendly. I was really kind of amazed that total strangers from all over the country were acting like they knew me already. And you know? That's really important. I think it's more intertwined because I get nervous before I race, and I feel exhilarated afterward. When I'm done, I'm like, "Wow, that was fun!" So, both of them are part of what keeps me going.

Barb echoed another theme I heard from most EALs. They understand the value of Community for how it enhances fun and engagement and helps us deal with the inevitable anxiety and uncertainty of new territory. Because our brains hate uncertainty, they can shut down when we encounter new challenging frontiers, whether at the top of an unfamiliar icy racecourse or at the beginning of a new role. Faced with the unknown, our brain signals danger, which can send our bodies into freeze, fight, or flight mode.

In Community, however, as Barb and other EALs have described, the threat is quickly diminished, allowing our bodies and brains to settle down and move into the exhilarating state of anxious confidence.[17] We, of course, don't want to eliminate all anxiety or stress because it can put us in a state of high engagement and elevate our performance. At the same time, too much anxiety can overwhelm our confidence and hijack our amygdala, the part of the reptilian brain that sounds the alarm in high-stress threat situations.

Self-Efficacy in Community

One of the reasons that connectivity impacts performance is that it can foster a shift in our embodied state. Researchers conducted clinical tests and found that stress levels, as measured by the stress hormone cortisol, increased or decreased depending on the presence of a best friend.[18]

In additional studies relevant to business leaders and ski racers alike, researchers have found that those who viewed a slope in the presence of a friend estimated it to be less steep than those who viewed it alone. Even viewing the slope while thinking about a supportive friend had the same results.[19] EALs climb slopes every day, and our perceptions of their steepness can impact our belief in our ability to succeed, which impacts actual success.

You may be familiar with psychologist Albert Bandura's term "self-efficacy" based on his findings that people's belief in themselves was a strong predictor of success.[20] Such confidence is often built through observing and interacting with other people. The opposite is true for people in very isolating jobs, where loneliness and low satisfaction scores are common.[21] With so much evidence that we are less stressed and more effective when we feel connected, there is even more reason to foster Community at work.

Building Community Means Business

Career advisors have long coached us to network, network, network. We know we *should* do it—and not just when we experience transitions. Beyond the usual advice, more research now supports the value of making and building connections for business success.

Over the past few years, my colleagues and I have collected and analyzed the results of more than 1,000 respondents to the *Agility Shift Inventory*™, an assessment of the mindset, attitude, and behaviors that support overall agility in organizations.[22] We found that leaders across industries who intentionally expanded and diversified their Relational Web (their network of skills, knowledge, talent, and resources) or Community had higher overall agility scores and were more able to effectively make sense of what was happening when things don't go as planned, as illustrated by the findings in the graphic below.

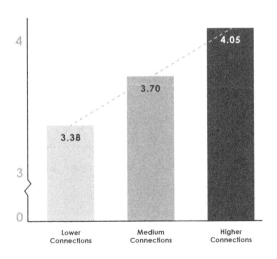

RELATIONAL WEB IMPACT

Intentionality about making and building connections significantly impacts overall agility.

These findings align with other recent research, such as the widely cited Google study of 180 teams.[23] They found that their most successful teams had leaders with the largest and most diverse social networks—one aspect of the Relational Web. These leaders were also intentional about making and building connections with others by doing things like regularly rotating with whom they ate lunch.

Shifting From Transactional to Relational Interactions

The business value of a relational approach inspired T-Mobile's Team of Experts strategy, led by Callie Field, President of the Business Group. This shift upended the traditional call center approach that left customers hanging on hold or being passed from department to department. Working in cross-functional "pods" with a specific account focus, this approach encourages collaboration, communication, and coordination of resources and resolutions among team members to respond to customer issues.

The shift at T-Mobile was from a transactional approach, in which the amount of time spent on a call was a key measure, to a relational approach, in which the resolution of customer issues is paramount. Field described the impact, "As a result, coaching conversations with reps often focus on the business impact of individual decisions and how a decision for a given customer will affect that customer's loyalty and the team's financial performance."

For example, in the past, a customer would have been told, "I'm really sorry about the inconvenience. Let me submit a ticket to engineering." Today would have a more relational interaction to a service outage, such as, "Yes, we're aware that a brush fire outside the city is affecting your service, and we're working on the issue. I've been in touch with the engineers on the ground, and they're working to restore service as we speak. They're telling me it should be up and running within 24 hours."[24]

This kind of relationality impacts employee as well as customer satisfaction. Call center turnover, notoriously high across industries, dropped an eye-popping 48% in the three years since the shift. And T-Mobile's customer satisfaction results consistently lead among the top four wireless carriers.[25] These shifts, however, cannot be taken for granted. After their integration with Sprint and the impact of the pandemic-induced talent shortage, T-Mobile is challenged, notably, along with their competitors. Continued renewal and reinvestment in a robust Community experience are critical for sustained results.[26]

Embodying Community

"Nobody's a dud!" exclaimed Dave "Chip" Norris, the then Group President of Alerus Financial. This positive energy is one of the main reasons he keeps coming back, week after week, year after year, braving the often-brutal conditions for the Ski Challenge racing series at Minnesota's Buckhill. "That's the frame of mind that everybody's in," he shared.

> We're doing something away from the normal, in the cold air, but you're dealing with a bunch of positive people. That's another reason it's just so energizing to me. We're all out there for the same reason, so you don't hang around any duds. That's another reason for doing it is just to be surrounded by that kind of attitude and energy, and it makes

the small irritations at work seem insignificant after you've been around a healthy element like that.

Chip beautifully describes what behavioral scientists have discovered: Fun is more fun with other people.[27] In controlled studies, researchers found that even activities that participants found inherently fun were even more engaging and energizing when done with others than alone. In other words, the game (and its four Ps of play, purpose, passion, and pleasure) is more fun if played in Community.

In a competitive talent market, these factors can make the difference between in-demand contributors staying engaged and committed or moving on to organizations where they can co-create a dynamic future.[28] Once again, the motivating relational energy of Community requires intentional leadership by EALs. Even more critical, through the upheavals of the pandemic, researchers found that leaders with "positive relational energy: the energy exchanged between people" helped to uplift, enthuse, and renew others. These EALs serve as "positive energizers [who] produce substantially higher levels of engagement, lower turnover, and enhanced feelings of well-being among employees."[29]

Leading with Relational Energy

The positive relational energy generated through the intentional co-creation of Community is embodied energy. Researchers Emma Seppälä and Kim Cameron report that this is "partly because at the cellular level of brain activity, cortical thickness is enhanced through exposure to relational energy, hormones such as oxytocin and dopamine are increased, and at the cellular level in the body, inflammation is reduced and immunity to disease is enhanced."[30] Unlike other efforts that can deplete us, interacting with those who embody positive relational energy enhances and sustains our own energy. This energy multiplies as EALs share their positive relational energy with others.

Chip shared how this positive relational energy creates results on the race hill and in business, "I tell you what, it's a lot easier to talk yourself into being the worst skier on the hill—that's no problem at all. You don't have to work hard to be a lousy skier and allow your attitude to steer you in that direction. You might as well have it steer you the other way." He went on to describe how he demonstrates this as an EAL with the leaders he coaches at his firm:

> I'll tell them that I will exaggerate to make my point. Then I'll role-play walking into somebody's office with no confidence. I'll use terrible body language, and I'll go over a proposal I'm pitching, and I almost apologize for it. Then, I'll turn around and walk back in with exactly the same information, with a completely different attitude and get to a totally different outcome.
>
> It's the same at the starting gate for a race. I can be the same skier, the same two legs, the same two arms, same everything when I get into that starting gate, but I can have a very, very different result based on my attitude. It's the same thing at work. I've done it with people. I've walked in and presented the exact same proposal twice just to show people how terrible a deal it can seem with one attitude and what a terrific solution it can seem with a different attitude.

Embodying Community, as Chip does, fosters a positive relational energy that others want to be a part of and amplify. Recruited to lead and grow the Twin Cities office, Chip started out with just three direct reports and zero assets under management. With his Embodied Agile Leadership, he grew the region to 600 employees and $1.2 billion in assets. The numbers are impressive by any measure, but even more meaningful to Chip and most EALs are the relationships they create along the way.

These relationships are more motivating than any pot of gold. While proud of his accomplishments in business, Chip values the people who co-create and share in his success even more. He summarized the power of Community when he told me, "Whenever I hear anybody say, 'If only I could win the lottery,' I tell them we already have."

COACHING

Find, Participate in, and Co-Create Community

All EALs want to continue to improve their performance and foster an environment where others can grow and thrive. They understand the power of positive relational energy in Community. They seek it out, actively participate in it, and encourage others to do the same. Use the questions below to discover how to be more intentional in your embodied participation in Community in ways that align with the Meaningful Identity you described in Chapter 4 and engage with the four Ps you identified in Chapter 1.

Download the *Embodied Reflection and Action Journal* with all of the coaching prompts, as well as additional resources here: https://pamela-meyer.com/staying-in-the-game-resources/ or use the QR code on the left.

What? *Practicing Embodied Awareness and Assessment*	• What are you learning in response to your reflections and actions from prior iterations, so far? • When and where have you experienced positive relational energy of Community in your game? • What were you doing? • With whom were you playing? Where were you playing?
Gut? *Engaging Your Whole Person*	• Close your eyes for a moment and envision yourself enjoying the positive relational energy of Community. What are you feeling on an emotional, physical, and even spiritual level?
So What? *Making Sense and Prioritizing*	• If you described a range of experiences of Community that fulfill various aspects of the four Ps for you, which are most relevant to or aligned with your life today? • Which experiences of Community are most engaging and energizing to you and most sustaining to your experience of livelihood? • If time or resources are constrained, which experiences of Community do you want to prioritize?
Now What? *Making Decisions and Acting*	With the embodied experience of Community in mind, how might you begin or continue to find, participate in, and co-create Community experiences for yourself and others? • **Find**: Who shares similar levels of enthusiasm and engagement in the four Ps of your game? Where and how do they connect? How do they share resources and exchange ideas? • **Participate**: What barriers might you remove, or what support do you need to participate in Community? • **Co-Create**: How can you contribute to the shared success and sustainability of Community? How might you practice "radical hospitality" to help others feel welcomed and included? What can you learn from others who are different from you? How can you help expand access to and diversify the Communities you enjoy? • What new habits or practices will help you sustain your progress?

CHAPTER 7

COMPETITION

Learning for Life

EMBODIED AGILE LEADERSHIP

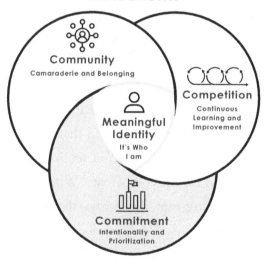

Community and Competition are nearly inseparable for Embodied Agile Leaders (EALs). In the last chapter, you learned how Community fosters engagement, energy, and performance and helps us construct and sustain our Meaningful Identity. In this chapter, you will discover the symbiotic relationship between Competition, Community, and Meaningful Identity and how together they spur many EALs to play the game at the highest level.

> I need the Community. I need somebody to push me farther than I would push myself. Because if I go out for a run, I'm gonna go for a mile and then be like, "All right, I'm done."
>
> —**Melissa Koenig**, multisport athlete and Director of Instructional Technology

The desire to get out there in Community and earn the rewards that come with winning is just one dimension that makes Competition such a compelling dynamic for EALs. You are likely familiar with the saying, "competition is for the competent." While Competition and competence share the same root, they are not the same. This is because having competence or a particular ability does not necessarily translate into performance. If this were the case, athletes could simply submit their resumes and not bother to show up on race day. Performance thrives in Community, which provides the engagement of Competition and accountability.

In business, sport, and all endeavors in life, being able to translate our skills, knowledge, and talent into performance when the stakes are high is the true test of ability. Of course, engaging in these tests, sometimes falling short of our aspirations, and the desire to do better next time keeps us coming back to perform again. It is what keeps EALs engaged in continuous learning and improvement. Understanding the dimensions of Competition can help us be more intentional in translating competence into performance.

Discover What Drives You

EALs are motivated by two forms of Competition, often in combination: extrinsic and intrinsic. When extrinsic Competition is the strongest driver, EALs have set their sights on external rewards, outcomes, and benchmarks, often competing against others. When the prevailing motivation is intrinsic Competition, it is because the experience itself and the opportunity for continuous improvement and learning that come with it are the more compelling rewards, which means EALs are largely in competition with themselves.

> I want to beat them, and they want to beat me. But if they see something I'm doing wrong, they'll tell me. Or if I can help them out, I'll tell them.
>
> —**Lilla Andrews, 82-year-old ski racer, Winter World Masters Games Gold Medalist**

Setting up camp in only one territory without understanding its context and interdependency with other territories would be a mistake. For example, studies show how feeling connected to a group (or Community) deepens competitors' experience, which in turn, motivates their persistence and performance.[1] In other words, if you are singularly focused on the outcome of a Competition without interacting with or enjoying the camaraderie of your fellow competitors (Community members), you might very well miss out on their support and cheerleading, which can affect your performance. Even if you achieve your goals in a given competition, you are less likely to persist and sustain that performance over time without finding a compelling intrinsic motivation. Understanding the role each type of Competition plays in *your* game can go a long way in motivating you to stay in it.

Competing with Others

I'm in the starting gate at the Winter Park public NASTAR course next to seven-year-old Tallulah who is wearing a pink tutu over her snow pants. I know her name is Tallulah because her parents call out to her to cheer her on as we get set to race on our parallel courses. I momentarily wonder how much more interesting my life might have been had my parents named me Tallulah (not to mention how much higher my search engine rankings would be). Without delay, the race official in the start house counts us down "3-2-1, Go!" and we both push off. I skate through the first few gates to gain as much speed as possible to carry into the rest of the course. Midway down, I can't help but glance over to the other course to track the pink tutu. I am relieved when I cross the finish line a full 10 seconds ahead. Yes, I remember how many seconds. I'm not proud of this. I then wait for her in the finish area to give her a fist bump and say, "You did awesome!"

My love of Competition, shared by EALS everywhere, includes all the energy, contradictions, and complexities embodied in racing Tallulah. Derived from the Latin verb *competere*, to compete means "to meet, come together." Competition most commonly involves two or more individuals or teams coming together in a contest. When I asked ski racer Dick Cole, who proudly races on both his snowboard and alpine skis well into his 80s, how important winning was to him, he replied, "It's everything!" He is unabashed in celebrating his success on the race hill and is excited to share it. Dick's extrinsic rewards gather meaning when they are shared with his wider Community. "I carry my medals around," he exclaimed and proudly shares them with anyone interested in hearing stories of his most recent successes.

Competing with Purpose and Play

EALs in business agree that achieving results is also critical to staying motivated and engaged over the long haul. In their research of individual contributor and team engagement, Harvard's Theresa Amabile and Steven Kramer found that even incremental progress toward shared goals and acknowledgment of accomplishments can make the difference between perseverance through obstacles and demoralized derailment.[2] Acknowledgment of progress not only amplifies the meaning and purpose of our efforts but also makes it more enjoyable, two critical ingredients for long-term engagement.

Our need to feel we are making progress and have that progress acknowledged by others is also at the center of one of the most important bodies of work in the psychology of motivation and well-being. Researchers Richard Ryan and Edward Deci were curious about the psychological needs that must be satisfied for people of all ages to thrive in learning, play, and work. In their earliest experiments,[3] they saw how those who had become solely attached to an extrinsic motivation for their performance soon lost interest and tended not to persevere in the face of obstacles when that external reward was removed, whereas those who stayed engaged had three basic psychological needs met:

- **Autonomy:** an experience of free will and the ability to make choices that impact how and what we do, even if within constraints
- **Competence:** an experience of early success or incremental progress toward competence and the possibility of mastery
- **Relatedness:** an experience of connectedness with others and that the endeavor has meaning in relation to others

These three elements are at the heart of self-determination theory (SDT),[4] which emerged from Ryan and Deci's research and have informed and impacted everything from how educators design learning experiences to how managers support team success. Flexible, self-guided learning options are now commonly woven into many learning programs from childhood through executive leadership development.

Competing with Agility

The groundswell movement toward self-organizing agile teamwork is a natural evolution of SDT. Agile teams plan, organize, and prioritize their work into short, iterative cycles, after which they pause to reflect on, learn from, and celebrate their progress. This autonomy and relatedness allow agile teams to Compete in a way that aligns with at least two of the game's four Ps: purpose and play.

EALs on agile teams articulate their purpose early and often. Through communication with their stakeholders, including their customers, they discover which elements of value are most significant.[5] By understanding what their stakeholders value, they can align their priorities with a shared purpose. For example, if my client values actionable insights over detailed reports, my team can self-organize to deliver that value.

The ability to Compete through self-organization is a form of play. Understanding stakeholder priorities or goals gives EALs and their collaborators the freedom to align their passion, skills, knowledge, and talent in a mutually rewarding way. This focus and freedom inspire the team to play with new ideas while team members support each other by playing new roles and playing with available resources. Playing in this way allows for both the autonomy and relationality of self-determination theory while respecting the skills, knowledge, and talent of all the players to Compete at the top of their competence. Ryan and Deci found that when these needs are satisfied, we experience psychological well-being, along with the pleasure and passion that motivate us to stay in the game.

Competing With Self

> I'm not trying to beat another person. I'm trying to be faster and faster on the hill. And if somebody does it in 18 seconds and I do it in 19, yes, I want to get down to 18. So I guess I always have a goal of doing better when I'm going down a course. I guess that's just natural for me.
> —Lilla Andrews, 82-year-old ski racer

While I share the love and extrinsic motivation of stepping up on the podium and coming home with a medal, the EALs I work and compete with have taught me to value another type of Competition: competition with myself. Some competitors are highly motivated to beat their peers, while others, such as Chip Norris, the Alerus Group President, whom you met in Chapter 6, and Bryan Davis, an EAL you are about to meet, consider *themselves* their most formidable competitor. These EALs are more motivated by the goal of doing just a little better each time out of the gate. Chip shared how he practices this off the racecourse.

> Whatever my peak is here, whether I've reached it or not, I've already told myself it won't bother me when I start going the other way. Wherever you are, you can always benchmark yourself to be better, which doesn't have to be stressful. It should be an energizing and fun thing.

Recognizing the inevitable limitations on the horizon that come with age, Chip reflected, "It's going to happen, and so I tell myself, 'I'm going to keep chasing it. I'm going to keep chasing it because I still don't think I've had my best race. But if I have, and I never get there, it's going to be fun trying. But I still don't think I've had my best race.'"

Chip is among many EALs who are motivated by benchmarks for their own progress and by comparing themselves to others on the playing field. Even in a highly competitive business, such as financial services, when progress can be measured in relation to others, EALs stay in the game by raising the bar even higher.

No stranger to the constraints and Competition in financial services, Bryan Davis also learned to set the bar high early in life when he quarterbacked teams to success from grade school through college. Today, as head of VIU by HUB, an innovative digital insurance platform, he shared the philosophy that guides him.

I want first to play my best, and in the process, I want to win at the same time. My perspective is that you never want to base your standards on the environment you're in. Your standards must be higher and bigger than that. And to me, that's what I do in leadership. That's what I do in sports. That's what I do in business. Set your standards high because you can sit here and say, "Hey, I'm at organization X. They used to be mediocre." So I can come in here, be a little bit better than mediocre, and be great. That's why I'm always trying to push myself to higher standards if possible.

When your most worthy Competition is your past performance, coupled with the innate pleasure you derive from continuous learning and improvement, you are propelled by an infinite energy source: intrinsic motivation. Ryan and Deci found this true when they expanded on their initial research with their colleague Christopher Niemiec. Looking for factors that support sustained engagement, they studied college students in their first year after graduation. They discovered that recent grads who measured their success solely based on the achievement of extrinsic goals reported overall poorer psychological well-being. In comparison, those whose goals were intrinsically focused reported better psychological well-being.[6]

Similar studies in populations of all ages in business[7,8] and education[9,10] reinforce the value of finding a sustaining intrinsic aspiration to motivate you to stay in the game. Of course, you don't need to be a psychologist to know the importance of finding intrinsic motivation for continuous improvement; you have your experience to guide you. If you have ever used achieving a specific goal or reward (e.g., losing fifteen pounds by your high school reunion or winning the top sales award) as your motivation, you've likely experienced that motivation wane soon after the goal was achieved. When our primary focus is the external reward, our source of energy and engagement is also largely out of our control. A variety of factors can impact your performance on any given day. If you are motivated to continue only if you consistently step on the podium, you will soon be derailed by the inevitable setbacks.

Competing for Learning

The intrinsic value of learning and improvement is at the heart of Bryan Davis's practice of Embodied Agile Leadership. He shared that "this is where the great leaders separate themselves from the average or even subpar. I would say to my organization at this stage, 'we're not failing enough.' And so, when I do performance reviews, everybody will tell you what they did well." To shift the focus, Bryan starts his performance reviews by asking his leaders to "tell me what you messed up. Because if you haven't really disrupted anything and had setbacks in something, you're probably not trying hard enough." At the same time, he emphasized that this doesn't mean, "Okay, well, I don't have to have any accountability. I can just go mess up something. We're all kumbaya, and this is not a big deal."

Over the course of his impressive career, Bryan has observed and studied many leaders. He discovered, "The great leaders know how to find that balance between one extreme and the other. As a leader, you promote this environment of 'How do we find the positivity and accountability in failures?' And accountability could be like, 'Man, what should I learn to do differently?'"

It takes both courage and humility to model the continuous learning of Embodied Agile Leadership. EALs know this because they don't expect or invite their colleagues to venture into new territory they don't explore themselves.

Competing for Continuous Improvement

Older athletes (35+ in most sports, even younger in others) are called "masters." Many athletes and EALs I interviewed wanted to clarify that they weren't technically "masters" and emphasized that they were still learning. While most had been competing for years, often in sanctioned "masters" events, and had their share of regional and even national medals, they didn't think of themselves as having achieved "mastery." And that is precisely the point. They all see themselves *in the process* of mastering.

EALs are mastering the ability to get in and stay in the game. True mastery is not determined by our results at the end of any single competition, any more than at the end of a single quarter. It is determined by our ability to stay competitive year after year. Masters athletes, particularly those who have competed for years well past the age many expected them to be at the top of their game, have mastered not only their sport but also their ability to stay in the game.

Always Be Mastering

Perhaps subconsciously, EALs are practicing a tried-and-true sales trope. If you come from a sales background or spend time with those who do, you are likely familiar with the acronym ABC for "always be closing." Salespeople keep their eyes on the prize in every interaction with current and prospective clients. When it comes to sustaining leadership agility, the prize is staying in the game. For this reason, the EALs I study and work with all practice ABM for "always be mastering."

Barb Brumbaugh, a long-time masters ski racer and coach, described how she translates continuous improvement to her high-stakes work as an ICU nurse. "I'll do something at work, for example, a hydration assessment, and I look at it and say, 'Oh, I can do better than that.' And then I go and redo it. Whereas some people might say, 'Okay, it's done. Whatever.' That's a kind of competitiveness. And I carry it from my own rehab [as a stroke survivor] to work, exercise, and my skiing. It's an attitude of 'I can do better than that.'" Barb was a true EAL who sadly passed away in fall 2021. Her Commitment, Competitiveness, and engagement in Community were evident in the hundreds of Facebook posts memorializing her life and impact.

EALs share a commitment to continuous learning and improvement. They are always exploring and experimenting, never settling for "good-enough" results in any arena. More than most, these EALs are masters of mastering. They also know that their serious competitors are doing the same.

Embodying Competition

Tiffany Dotson first caught my attention at an event for area learning and development professionals at DePaul University's Center to Advance Education for Adults. She was the most engaged, charismatic, and active contributor in the room. Every time she spoke, she had a new and interesting insight or idea; when she wasn't speaking, she was actively listening, learning and building new connections. I soon discovered that Tiffany had been invited by her friend, a faculty member in her doctoral program at the time. Somehow, she made time for new learning and relationship-building while working at a major corporation in Chicago and finishing her doctorate at Columbia University, each more than a full-time endeavor on its own.

Over the next few years, I stayed in touch with the now Dr. Tiffany Dotson as she moved into leadership roles at Pfizer, JP Morgan Chase, and Liberty Mutual Insurance, where she is VP of Global Talent, Leadership, and Learning. Dr. Dotson was aggressively recruited because of her reputation for developing innovative learning programs that deliver business results. In this role, she oversees leadership development from strategy to execution for the 50,000 company employees and 7,000 managers around the globe. Dr. Dotson leads by embodying the spirit and practice of ABM through a relentless commitment to continuous learning.

Leading with Learning Agility

Leading in a large, complex, growing organization requires more than learning; it requires learning *agility*, or the ability to continuously learn, adapt, and perform effectively in unfamiliar situations. Studying the career arcs of executives across domains, researchers Robert W. Eichinger and Michael M. Lombardo found that learning agility was a better predictor of promotability and success after a promotion than other indicators, including IQ.[11] They found that those without learning agility, up to 70% of even those identified as having high potential, can be successful within their comfort zone but soon derail when thrown into new situations for which they have no experience. In contrast, learning agile leaders like Dr. Dotson have developed a Meaningful Identity and are intrinsically motivated to lead with ongoing curiosity, intentional learning, and adaptation.

During her formative years in Chicago, Dr. Dotson shared that she quickly discovered her values and value through experiences and contexts that validated her Meaningful Identity. "I experienced my power in front of a group as early as kindergarten, giving a speech in front of the room and later on in the debate team and cheerleading squad. I loved performing and the positive feedback I received. It felt good. And I had good grades, too. So, I had early evidence of my value."

Many EALs who generously shared their stories and insights, like the leaders you met in Chapter 5, trace their passion and purpose to their formative years. Whether or not they were aware of the impact at the time, as adults, they all embrace their early experiences as an important part of their leadership narrative. Dr. Dotson's purpose has been crystal clear ever since she can remember:

> It's been my mission in life: helping people think better to design their own lives as opposed to living by default. When I show up at a meeting and say to my staff, 'here's what I'm learning,' it puts them at ease and helps them get in the same mindset. Our goal isn't perfection; it's continuous learning and growth.

In increasingly dynamic environments, a growing number of leaders at all levels of organizations are developing or demonstrating their ability to lead with learning agility. They are discovering what Dr. Dotson and other EALs have—that modeling continuous learning and improvement instills their colleagues with the confidence to perform at their best under pressure and uncertainty.

Create Space for Continuous Learning

No one can effectively learn, let alone engage and innovate if they are protecting their image or operating out of fear. It is like trying to drive with the brakes on. Agile leaders embody humility by sharing what they are learning and asking others to share their new learning and discoveries. In addition, EALs seek out new experiences and engage guides and coaches who can provide a good balance of support and challenge. We are much less likely to take risks if we experience a high degree of one without the other. As an EAL, you are responsible for embodying a demeanor and behaviors that inspire your colleagues to co-create an environment where all can thrive.

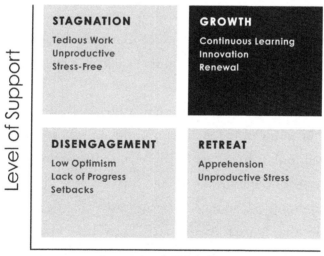

The challenge-support matrix above, introduced by Nevitt Sanford in 1966, is reflected in several growth models used in management and talent development today. An imbalance of challenge or support (too much or too little) can be a barrier to getting and staying in the game. The goal is to spend most of our time in the growth space, where we experience enough challenge to keep us engaged, curious, and creative, with enough support to persevere through the inevitable obstacles and setbacks. Growth space is not and should not be all sunshine and roses, but rather a provocative space that challenges us to examine our assumptions and vision of what is possible. In other words, growth space is also the brave space Desiree Adaway described in Chapter 5. Because, of course, growing often requires bravery.

Celebrate Progress, Not Perfection

For most EALs, at least equally important to standing on top of the podium is how they mark their progress along the way. The brain needs feedback to stay engaged and to stay motivated to continue improving; it needs *positive* feedback.[12,13] When this feedback happens in Community, it can amplify the impact and help reinforce Meaningful Identity.

Even small improvements warrant a literal or metaphorical fist bump in the finish area. The director of the British cycling team, Sir David Brailsford, is legendary for his focus on "marginal gains." He discovered that he and his team could exponentially improve results by making—and celebrating—1% improvements in a wide range of variables that impact performance. These have included sixteen gold medals in two Olympics, and seven Tour de France wins in eight years.[14]

EALs recognize progress in all the endeavors contributing to their ability to stay in the game. Progress includes new learning and incremental improvements, expanded capacity, mindset, enjoyment, and engagement in all its incarnations.

COACHING

Competing Through Continuous Learning and Growth

The prompts in this chapter's coaching will help you become more aware of your motivation for Competition and discover more opportunities to engage it for continued learning, improvement, and growth.

Download the *Embodied Reflection and Action Journal* with all of the coaching prompts, as well as additional resources here: https://pamela-meyer.com/staying-in-the-game-resources/ or use the QR code on the left.

What? *Practicing Embodied Awareness and Assessment*	• What am I learning in response to my reflections, actions, and experiments so far? • Thinking about the spectrum of your motivation for playing the game from intrinsic to extrinsic, where would you place yourself today? **Intrinsic** ⟵⟶ **Extrinsic** | Intrinsic	Extrinsic
• The experience itself • New learning and growth • Greater sense of belonging • Competing with myself	• Achieving results • Recognition • Tangible rewards and awards • Competing with others | • Considering where you placed yourself, what is it about those rewards that is most significant to you?
Gut? *Engaging Your Whole Person*	• What are you feeling (physically, emotionally, and otherwise) when you experience yourself at your best in Competition? • What more does your body tell you about how Competition is important to you?
So What? *Making Sense and Prioritizing*	This stage of embodied reflection invites you to become aware of how the experience of Competition you have just described is relevant to your current life and values. • If you described a range of experiences of Competition that fulfill various aspects of the four Ps (play, purpose, passion, and pleasure), which are most relevant to or aligned with your life today? • Which experiences of Competition are most engaging and energizing to you and most sustaining to your experience of livelihood? • If time or resources are constrained, which experiences of Competition do you want to prioritize?

Now What? *Making Decisions and Acting*	• With your understanding of Competition in mind, and your embodied experience and priorities, how might you set yourself up for success to compete at your best? • Are there any obstacles getting in the way of your success? • How can you or who/what can you engage to help remove these obstacles? • With these insights in mind, what actions can you take, or activities do you want to prioritize and invest in, to heighten and sustain your experience of Competition and the rewards that come with it? • What new habits or practices will help you sustain your progress?

CHAPTER 8

COMMITMENT

Prioritizing, Persevering, and Adapting

EMBODIED AGILE LEADERSHIP

- **Community** — Camaraderie and Belonging
- **Competition** — Continuous Learning and Improvement
- **Meaningful Identity** — It's Who I am
- **Commitment** — Intentionality and Prioritization

While working full-time as an engineer with the Army Corps of Engineers, Mike "Geronimo" Lanier was ski racing 140 days a year at his peak. He described his Commitment as, "I'm either all in or on the sidelines," For Mike, Commitment means action. "I immediately sought out racing instruction and groups of people who raced. I actually got into masters racing early, even before I knew how to race." For Mike, "all in" also meant finding and co-creating Community, searching out local and national Competitions, and working hard to understand what it meant to be competitive.

While Mike's story stands out, even among the most active and engaged Embodied Agile Leaders (EALs), his clarity of focus and purpose is echoed across the spectrum. Put simply, EALs make playing the game a priority. And they understand and prioritize all the elements necessary to get in it and stay in it—whatever "it" is. In whatever setting they play and however EALs name their game, they all describe a level of Commitment and ability to prioritize, persevere, and adapt through disruptions and setbacks, large and small.

Commitment Is Motivation + Discipline

Commitment means prioritizing what you care about. It requires motivation and discipline. Just ask Mike. He will tell you that, while not the same, motivation and discipline are interrelated. Motivation is the spark of enthusiasm that propels us into action. Everyone has days when our enthusiasm flags or we experience doubts or lack focus and motivation. On those days, we practice discipline.

Discipline grows from our ability to regulate and engage our embodied experience for specific purposes or goals. Developing consistent habits is an effective way to practice discipline. For example, I've developed a habit of starting most days with a series of exercises that I call my "warm-up." It's not so rigorous that it drains me, but it's enough to jump-start my metabolism and truly "warm up" for the day ahead. I'm not gonna lie. I don't always feel like starting my day this way. When I haven't slept well or have a lot of work on my plate, I am tempted to head to my desk and get to work. On these days, rather than argue with myself or indulge in excuses for why "just today" it would be okay to skip my warm-up, I tap into discipline and my habitual routine. Similar habits help me stay consistent with my writing and other activities that require regular, intentional engagement to make progress. In this way, discipline and motivation support each other. Without such practices, we would be at the mercy of the day's mood, energy level, or current distraction. Of course, you should not be held hostage to a set routine.

Committing for Engagement

Companies make considerable investments in surveying and trying to improve employee engagement. Why? Because engagement is often linked to a range of performance indicators.[1,2] The term "engagement" is broadly associated with employee enthusiasm; work motivation; and alignment with organizational vision, mission, values, and purpose. When we experience synchronicity between an organization's goals and our Meaningful Identity, we are much more likely to be intrinsically motivated to contribute more for shared success.

The promise of engagement aligned with purpose starts during the recruiting process. At H&M, the long-time commitment to sustainable fashion is an essential differentiator for customers and prospective employees alike. Chris Mikulski, whom you met earlier, shared, "If we can get you on the phone for your first interview, then you usually want to join our company because we are values-driven, taking our responsibilities and commitment to people and planet very seriously, pioneering the future of the fashion industry. These are great things that people want to be a part of."

Organizations like H&M work to avoid the potential shadow side of personal interests becoming overly entwined with the interests of an organization. For example, an imbalance of Commitment that benefits a business can masquerade as "high engagement" but can come at steep personal costs to employees, ultimately diminishing the rewards for all over time. Employees can experience negative impacts on family and other meaningful relationships, as well as on mental and physical health. Organizations also suffer when the pace and pressure are unsustainable. Even highly engaged employees can become demoralized and experience burnout. When this happens, your top talent may be motivated in another direction: the exit.

With such high stakes, EALs lead with embodied awareness to avert the possibility of Commitment becoming unsustainable. By paying attention to their own and their colleagues' well-being, they measure success well beyond the bottom line.

Commitment and Community

Commitment is rooted in coming together and supporting each other. While often thought of as an individual endeavor, particularly in Western culture that glorifies personal achievement, Commitment shares the same "com" root of togetherness as Community and Competition. With a similar Latin origin as the other dynamics, *committere* means "to unite, connect, or bring together."

You may have experienced the impact of the mistaken emphasis on individual Commitment firsthand. If you have ever made a commitment that you fully intended to keep but found it hard to stick with over time, especially if your friends, family, or colleagues didn't share your priorities, you know the value of Community. Commitments made without engagement in Community are much more difficult to maintain. Whether it be consistency in adopting a meditation practice, healthy eating habits, regular exercise, being a better communicator, or other intentional practices, research shows that doing so while connected to others can be a critical factor in long-term success.[3]

For many EALs, initial participation in the game may *start* as a solo endeavor or casual exploration, as when I happened upon that first public racecourse while skiing in Colorado. However, once reengaged, I was inspired to seek out others who shared the same passion. In the Community of my regional race teams, it became much easier to maintain a Commitment to all it took to improve my performance and stay in the game.

Fostering Commitment Within Community in Your Organization

High-performance organizations are filled with passionate leaders. For these EALs, the autonomy, competence, and relatedness that motivate engagement also fuel sustained Commitment.[4] Building on the power of self-determination (introduced in Chapter 7), Norwegian researchers found that sustained Commitment is fostered through social connections and the intrinsic reward of continuous improvement.[5] These two dimensions lead to social validation or recognition, as many EALs have described across settings. In practice, this means that organizations that help people build connections and opportunities for social recognition help EALs prioritize the aspects of Competition that enable long-term Commitment.

Committing for Agility

Appreciating the link between Commitment and Community is critical to sustained success for organizations that need to build their capability and capacity for agility. Relatedness is woven into all aspects of Agile frameworks and the Agile Transformations (the scaled use of Agile frameworks and practices) that are being practiced to at least some degree in 94% of organizations today.[6] Agile Transformations are founded on the understanding that we make sense of what is happening and get work done most effectively with and through other people.

The need to Commit for agility is especially acute for rapidly evolving environments, such as healthcare. Recognizing the dynamic complexity of their environment sparked UCB's Agile Transformation that James Hlavenka, Esq., whom you met in Chapter 5, was recruited to help design and lead. UCB and businesses working across complex sectors are committing for agility and doing so by embracing several best practices. For example, Scrum, the most popular framework, is guided by a series of "ceremonies" ensuring Commitment is sustained through Community.

Agile Transformations are founded on the understanding that we make sense of what is happening and get work done most effectively with and through other people.

Committing to Sustainable Value

Because agile ways of working commit to delivering customer value *and* being sustainable for all participants, most critical processes and decisions happen within Community—in this case, the team. Each new work cycle begins with a planning session that reviews the customer/stakeholder priorities, breaks down the elements of the project, identifies those that will deliver the greatest value, assesses the capacity of the team, and agrees on the criteria for completion (what is considered "done" for each element). Commitments are then made, and accountability is established in a variety of forums, including:

- **Daily Stand-Ups:** short (15 minutes or less) meetings in which team members share their progress, regroup, and identify obstacles they need help removing
- **Sprint Reviews:** longer meetings (typically 1–4 hours) to reflect on the product, service development progress, or the user or market input, and then revise priorities for the next working cycle
- **Retrospectives:** meetings (also lasting 1–4 hours) that focus on amplifying team strengths, surfacing lessons learned, and applying them to improve team capabilities, and the working process going forward

Similar to the workout rituals that sustain progress and performance for masters athletes, the practices of Agile teams ensure sustained Commitment to customer and stakeholder value, a critical performance indicator in business. It may or may not make sense for you to adopt an Agile framework in your business. It does make sense to pay attention to the lessons learned from EALs who are thriving through their Commitment to collaborate sustainably within Community.

Prioritizing

Newton's first law of motion also describes the challenge (and opportunity) faced by all EALs who prioritize staying in the game for the long haul. According to Newton's law, "a body at rest tends to stay at rest, and a body in motion tends to stay in motion unless acted on by an external force."[7]

Dick Cole, the ski and snowboard racer who continues in Competition (and wins) well into his 80s, is passionate and unequivocal about prioritizing his health and fitness practices. "It's a commitment. An absolute necessity. You just gotta do it. If you don't, you're gonna die." Setting such life-and-death stakes can undoubtedly create a sense of urgency to motivate aspiring EALs to do what it takes to get and stay ready for Competition and to participate in Community. However, as I've shared previously, research shows that positive, rather than punitive, aspirations are more effective in sustaining long-term engagement.[8] For example, thinking about how much fun it is to be out there participating with friends, spending an exhilarating day skiing with family, or even heading out solo and enjoying countless chance encounters on chairlift rides may be more inspiring than fear of an early demise.

> "It's a commitment. An absolute necessity. You just gotta do it. If you don't, you're gonna die."

With a positive focus, EALs tap into the energy of creating value and impact for their stakeholders. When this value is aligned with the four Ps of their game, it is much easier for EALs to prioritize the decisions and actions that are most likely to create it.

RE-Prioritizing for a Dynamic Future

When the future is stable and predictable, we can assess the situation, set our priorities, and get to work with confidence. There's just one catch. The future is never stable; it is dynamic. If you remember a time in your life when you were confident that the future was stable and predictable, my guess is that you are likely thinking of a time when you were living in a comfortable bubble that gave you the illusion of stability and predictability rather than the reality. Likely at some point, that bubble was burst by something unexpected and unplanned, whether in your personal or professional life or by something larger beyond your control, such as a natural disaster or a geopolitical upheaval. For this reason, prioritizing is not a "set it and forget it" endeavor. No matter your level of comfort and confidence in your plan, something will come along to disrupt it.

Living and working in the reality of a dynamic future, EALs don't so much prioritize but constantly *re-*prioritize in response to change and new discoveries. Software developers discovered the folly of making detailed plans decades ago. Constantly changing requirements and user needs did not lend themselves to investing in detailed plans, let alone to marshaling the resources to execute them. Spurred by these discoveries, most organizations are moving away from linear "waterfall" ways of working in which projects are planned in detail up front when the least is known about the future.

Committing to Fast Feedback

The wide adoption of agile ways of working described earlier allows organizations to quickly respond to empirical evidence discovered through regular work cycles (sprints) characterized by experimentation and prototyping. These fast feedback loops allow for rapid learning and adapting while minimizing the risk of errors and waste or of simply missing the mark. This also maximizes value because the customer or user is providing feedback at each iteration, ensuring that what they value is prioritized.

New product developers use fast feedback to make positive changes in each iteration. You don't have to adopt an Agile framework to benefit from its best practices. EALs across domains have learned the value of fast feedback loops. Masters athletes love fast feedback because they can incorporate it into their next loop through the training course; employees are also most likely to improve their performance with timely feedback. EALs seek fast feedback and use their learning to improve their performance as leaders.

Committing to Outcomes, Not Output

The Commitment, then, for EALs is not to execute the "plan" but to prioritize and re-prioritize the creation and delivery of value. This means that EALs make a Commitment to their outcome rather than to their output. One way to understand the distinction between the two is to imagine a time when you or a loved one had a health challenge. You most likely placed greater value on the outcome of your care team's efforts than on whether the team checked all the boxes on the original diagnostic protocol, despite new discoveries. The same is true for your stakeholders. They are less concerned about how well you followed the original plan, than whether you delivered value. The only way to ensure this is to Commit to re-prioritizing in response to new learning.

Persevering

"Don't give up," counseled another long-time masters racer as we shared a short chairlift ride back up to the start of the racecourse at tiny Wilmot Mountain in Wisconsin. He had asked the universal chairlift ride opening question, "So, how is your day going so far?" and offered this simple encouragement after I shared that I was frustrated with my skiing that season. Despite all my training, I wasn't seeing better results. In the few minutes we were together, my fellow racer said that he totally understood and was just now starting to emerge from his recent year-long slump. "Don't give up," he repeated as we raised our ski tips to off-load and skated over to line up for the next run. That simple encouragement helped me persevere through the rest of the season and finish strong.

> **"Don't give up."**

The ability to not give up and to keep getting out there is especially important when we are tempted to "stay at rest." Dick Cole shared how he coaches himself on such days. "Of course, there are days I don't want to get out there at 6 am. My bed is warm, and it's 10° out. I have a conversation with myself, 'Wouldn't it be nice to just stay here?' Then [I say to myself], 'No. Nope. Just get out there. Gotta do it.'"

People who get out there in all conditions, decade after decade, have grit. Described by researcher Angela Duckworth as "passion and perseverance toward long-term goals,"[9] she expands:

> Grit isn't talent. Grit isn't luck…instead, grit is about having what some researchers call an "ultimate concern"—a goal you care about so much that it organizes and gives meaning to almost everything you do. And grit is holding steadfast to that goal. Even when you fall down. Even when you screw up. Even when progress toward that goal is halting or slow.

People who persevere are not easily derailed by obstacles and setbacks. They find a way to recover, regroup, reenergize, and refocus on their goals and passion. Persevering often includes tapping the power of the other "coms." Remembering that you are part of a Community that will miss you when you are not present and that you desire to stay in the Competition with others and to continue learning and improving can help your setback become the start of your comeback.

Persevering also means not waiting for someone else to inspire or motivate you. Abbie More, Product Group Manager and ski instructor, whom you first met in Chapter 4, shared, "In business, you have to take responsibility. If you have a challenge in business, if there's an account you just can't get into, take ownership of it. Don't sit back and say, 'Well, they won't take my calls.' Figure out how to make it happen."

Embodying Perseverance—and Knowing When Not to Persevere

Sticking with Commitment requires endurance. Self-described Black, lesbian, mother, warrior, and poet Audre Lorde wrote why endurance is so critical to realize purpose:

> We can learn to work and speak when we are afraid in the same way we have learned to work and speak when we are tired. For we have been socialized to respect fear more than our own needs for language and definition, and while we wait in silence for that final luxury of fearlessness, the weight of that silence will choke us.[10]

Lorde was not suggesting that we abuse ourselves for the cause of positive change but instead reminds us that we can persevere and overcome social-emotional barriers in the same way we have learned to push through physical barriers. Sports coaches call the ability to persevere "mental toughness," while researchers call it "endurance work."

In their study of the endurance work of high-altitude mountaineers, researchers found that climbers learn to become keenly aware of their embodied experiences during expeditions. Mountaineers' ability to slow down enough to interpret their bodily sensations to make them meaningful, before responding to them can be the difference between returning to base safely or leaving it all on the mountain.[11]

Awareness of their embodied experience also allows mountaineers to reengage with their motivating purpose and to push past their pain and exhaustion when their mindset is the most formidable obstacle. At such decision points, researchers found that mountaineers also learned to make intentional choices to forge on by thinking about all they had invested in the goal of reaching the summit. This awareness and interpretation of experience is the intentional practice of "endurance work" and is as necessary for negotiating an unexpected boulder as overcoming resistance in the boardroom.

With an embodied awareness of our physical sensations, our mental and emotional state, as well as the wider social dynamics and relevant environmental factors, we have a much better chance of not falling prey to the attachment to our original plan just because it was *the plan*.

Adapting

Commitment to embodied awareness can be particularly challenging when the stakes are high. Few environments have higher stakes than fighter jet cockpits. I've been lucky enough to learn more about the trust and communication demanded in this environment from retired US Air Force fighter pilot and current masters race coach Graham Smith. He shared that each time he buckled into the cockpit as lead pilot on his tactical reconnaissance missions in Vietnam, his core focus was on being present and "supporting my wingmen so we all come home."

Committing to Preparing, Not Planning

In this environment, while pilots take off with a flight plan and mission, they are trained to beware of "plan continuation bias." Attachment to a set plan can bias decision-making by filtering out critical new information that doesn't confirm the plan. Graham shared the life-or-death stakes of Embodied Agile Leadership in the cockpit, "If you didn't pay attention to what you were doing, you became a target." This meant a highly attuned "situational awareness" in which he and his fellow pilots were trained to keep their heads on a constant swivel because "you not only needed to know where you were headed but what might be headed at you." Graham recounted the harrowing maneuvers he led to evade enemy heat-seeking missiles. No plan could save them when a surface-to-air missile had locked into their jet engine exhaust. "You were always relying on the other guy's eyes and in a constant state of readiness to change course."

Few EALs in business experience the stakes of the fighter jet cockpit. However, they can learn lessons from these elite air force teams by shifting their focus from planning to preparing. Executives are learning to hold their plans lightly and shift their mission in response to incoming data, trends, and other unplanned events. Many use the OODA loop, which stands for observe, orient, decide, and act. A decision cycle developed for rapid decision-making on the battlefield by US Air Force Colonel John "Forty-Second" Boyd, the OODA loop is also used by many EALs in business and other high-stakes fields.

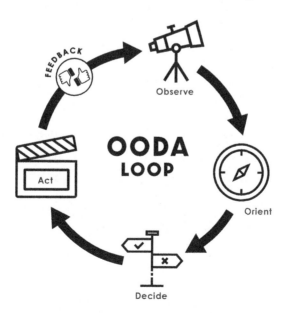

In increasingly complex and sometimes incomprehensible contexts, EALs know they cannot always rely solely on critical thinking skills, analytical capabilities, prior knowledge, or experience to make sense of what is going on to adapt and reprioritize for action.

Collaborating and Deciding with Embodied Awareness

When the stakes are high, the present context is VUCA (volatile, uncertain, complex, and ambiguous) and the future is dynamic, our embodied awareness can be our most reliable source of information for the first two stages of OODA—observe and orient. This is especially true when we need to discern the truth in a sea of conflicting or biased information sources or those sources with unreliable track records. We must know what we are experiencing, including our body sensations, mental and emotional state, social dynamics, and environment, and make sense of these experiences before acting.

Preparing, not planning, increases the likelihood that you will be responsive, not reactive when the stakes are high.

From the moment they step off the bus at the US Air Force Academy, new cadets learn to commit to the success of their fellow airmen and women. Graham shared, "from day one, we were taught we must cooperate to graduate." It doesn't matter if you are the best and brightest if you can't communicate, collaborate, and coordinate. Using core tenets of cockpit resource management, pilots rapidly assess and interpret all relevant inputs and check their biases in communication with their crew members and air traffic control, using four verbal exchanges:[12]

- I need to talk to you.
- I listen to you.
- I need you to talk to me.
- I expect you to talk to me.

When the stakes are high, trust and communication are anything but a "soft skill," as some business leaders have termed it. Graham shared his experience leading tight formations of wingmen, sometimes flying 3 feet apart and 50 feet above the ground to evade radar. He told me that some jets at the time had a second seat for the GIB, which I was surprised to learn stands for the "Guy in Back" (more formally, the WSO or Weapons Systems Operator). "You have to have absolute trust. They have to trust me, and I have to trust them." Graham emphasized the stakes, "In that situation, as the lead pilot, I can't make any maneuver my wingmen can't follow. There is no room for error."

The nonnegotiable mutual trust that Graham described is critical to the four exchanges. Committing to preparing rather than planning heightens the ability to succeed. Trust and real-time communication also ensure that pilots accurately assess their current reality as they move into the next two stages of OODA—decide and act. In a state of readiness, EALs are prepared to shift direction in response to all inputs not anticipated in the original plan.

Bounce Forward

In ski racing and many other sports, "falling" is not just a metaphor. Actually, we don't fall; we crash (trust me, I know). Masters athletes are no different from others around the globe. During the upheaval and uncertainty of the pandemic years, illness, job loss or shifts, financial setbacks, and family stress were just a few of the challenges that affected all of us. We all expect to stumble or worse. But just as with all comeback stories, the interesting part is not how we lost our balance but how we got back up.

Staying in the game through these experiences requires adaptability or the ability to "bounce back." However, when you are staying in the game for the long haul, you cannot expect to always bounce back to your familiar baseline. More accurately, EALs make the mindset shift that enables them to "bounce forward" to the best version of themselves they can be now. Many masters athletes come back from ligament tears and joint reconstructions, along with other significant injuries and illnesses. In some cases, this means no longer competing in certain events or particularly challenging conditions or moving to a competition class that matches their current capabilities. In others, they come back even stronger and more agile, enabling them to be even more competitive.

In either case, the comeback process involves assessing your current capabilities and setting your sights on new possibilities. Barb Brumbaugh, the ICU nurse, beloved competitor, and race coach, focused on how she might adapt to her diminished capacity after a series of strokes left her with balance and mobility issues. Only days before she passed away, Barb was watching the Paralympics and posted on Facebook that she was setting her sights on a new goal, getting back in the game as a Paralympian. While she knew she might need to adapt to a new game, Barb never lost her Commitment or sense of identity as an EAL.

Committing for Progress

Commitment, then, is more about committing to being in it than how you are in it. EALs commit to progress through continuous learning aligned with an evolving Meaningful Identity. Focusing on the dynamic process of *committing* is much more likely to result in long-term success than latching on to a specific way of getting there.

In fact, shifting Commitment from a set routine to a flexible one can make all the difference in the likelihood of success and derailment. In their investigation of factors contributing to long-term Commitment to fitness practices, researchers recruited college students interested in improving their fitness discipline. The volunteers were divided into two groups: one that received an incentive to exercise within a set window several times a week and another that was rewarded for exercising anytime during the week. They found that those who were rewarded for keeping a specific routine soon fell off their Commitment. Members of the group given flexible incentives had learned to prioritize exercising itself, not the set routine, and adapted even when their schedule was disrupted. This pattern continued even after the incentives were removed and the participants were told the study was completed.[13]

Among the study participants, the latter group had learned to commit to and prioritize the *outcome* of sustaining their fitness rather than the *output* of maintaining a set schedule. This is a particularly important insight for leading and learning in a dynamic future where plans can shift at a moment's notice, quickly derailing scheduled Commitments. Whether your Commitment is to your fitness practices, professional development or to improving business results, make a Commitment to the outcome of the doing of it, not whether it happens every Thursday at 3 pm.

Embodying Commitment

Across playing fields, EALs prioritize, persevere, and adapt to maintain their Commitment. Their ability to lead with an embodied awareness and to quickly assess their current reality in communication with trusted colleagues sets them apart from those who derail when things don't go as planned. Prioritizing preparing over planning ensures the state of readiness to succeed in a dynamic future.

COACHING
Prioritizing, Persevering, and Adapting

With your Meaningful Identity in mind, as well as the four Ps of *your* game, reflect on this chapter's questions to clarify your Commitment and make the shift from planning to preparing. By prioritizing and re-prioritizing your available time, energy, and resources, you will improve your ability to persevere through obstacles and setbacks, and adapt to internal and external changes, to stay in the game.

Download the *Embodied Reflection and Action Journal* with all of the coaching prompts, as well as additional resources here: https://pamela-meyer.com/staying-in-the-game-resources/ or use the QR code on the left.

What? *Practicing Embodied Awareness and Assessment*	• What are you learning in response to your reflections, experiments, and actions so far? • What attitudes, activities, and habits have you adopted that support your Commitment, Meaningful Identity, and ability to stay in the game? • What Communities or other resources help you prioritize and enjoy these activities and habits?
Gut? *Engaging Your Whole Person*	• What are you feeling (physically, emotionally, and otherwise) when you are living into your Commitment? • What more does your body tell you about the value of Committing (prioritizing, persevering, and adapting)?
So What? *Making Sense and Prioritizing*	• How is the experience of Commitment that you have just described relevant to your current life and values? • How does Committing to staying in the game fit into or influence your whole life?
Now What? *Making Decisions and Acting*	• With your embodied experience of Commitment in mind, how might you set yourself up for success in committing to staying in the game? Specifically, how can you better practice prioritizing, persevering, and adapting? • What obstacles are getting in the way of your success? • How can you or who/what can you engage to help remove these obstacles? • With these insights in mind, what actions can you take or activities do you want to prioritize, and invest in, to heighten and sustain your Commitment and the rewards that come with it? • What new habits or practices will help you sustain your Commitment?

PART III
STAYING AND PLAYING FOR LIFE AND LIVELIHOOD

In Part I, you learned about the nature and value of the game, and in Part II, you discovered how Embodied Agile Leaders (EALs) live into their Meaningful Identity and how they co-create Community, where they enjoy the continuous learning and improvement of Competition and prioritize, persevere, and adapt through Commitment.

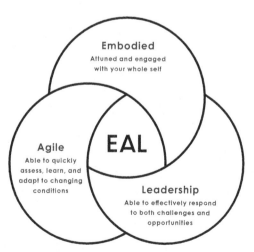

While Parts I and II primarily focused on getting in and *being* in the game, Part III is dedicated to additional themes and stories to inspire you to continue *staying* and playing for life and livelihood. Staying in the game means staying agile and relevant, strong and resilient, and happy.

Each of these practices offers fresh approaches while revisiting themes introduced in earlier chapters. This is by design. Many of the insights that help EALs find and get in their game also help them stay in their game. In the chapters ahead, you will discover how the mindset and practices of these EALs enable them to stay and play year after year.

CHAPTER 9

STAYING AGILE AND RELEVANT

Lilla Andrews, formerly Lilla Gidlow, learned long ago that staying relevant means staying agile. You can't have one without the other; both are crucial for sustained success. Still racing at age 82 in all alpine skiing disciplines, including high-speed downhill, she embodies agile leadership and engages the dynamics of Community, Competition, and Commitment to ensure she keeps playing.

Lilla's Meaningful Identity precedes her. She is not only a hero at her local ski area of Buck Hill, Minnesota (legendary as the early training ground of Olympic Gold Medalist and World Cup Champion Lindsey Vonn), but she also makes regular trips out west to compete with the Rocky Mountain Masters. In addition to her impressive collection of national medals, Lilla was the gold medalist in slalom and won bronze in giant slalom at the Winter World Masters Games in Innsbruck, Austria, in 2020. At age 79, she was the oldest woman participating in the Alpine Skiing event. In 2023 she received yet another honor—induction into the Minnesota Senior Sports Association Hall of Fame.

I knew all this before I was lucky enough to meet Lilla at a race camp at Copper Mountain. I didn't have to work hard to find her amid the helmeted, goggled, and masked skiers at the top of the course. A round of cheers erupted as she arrived in the start area for our first run. Lilla's sea of friends and fans high-fived her and cleared a path so she could slip into the start without waiting. The admiration and respect she receives are well deserved. As is true of every Embodied Agile Leader (EAL) you have met through these stories, Lilla's agility and relevancy are not an accident. "It's definitely my identity," she shared. Men far outnumber women in masters alpine racing, and her Meaningful Identity and ability to stay agile and relevant into her 80s are especially rare. I wanted to learn more.

After her win at the World Masters Games, Lilla was asked by a local TV reporter what motivates her to keep going. Her response was lighthearted, "I guess I don't know how to sit very well."[1] As I suspected and soon learned, the reality is more serious and intentional. It must be. No athlete can ignore their body, but an athlete who has lived in her body for 80-plus years must embody it with extra intentionality.

In addition to training and competing on snow six months of the year, Lilla works out independently and with a physical therapist because "I've had this nerve damage and don't have much feeling in my legs and feet." That last statement alone would be enough for many to step out of the game, let alone one that depends on lower body agility. It is just another opportunity for Lilla to adapt and find more ways to stay relevant in her sport. For example, she shared how older athletes can keep competing even when their bodies are not as responsive as they once were.

> There are ways you can pull back a little bit if you want to. You can go a little wider [around the gates] in the race.

... You can go back to the old-fashioned way, the reverse shoulder. Or [in slalom] cross-blocking, which I've done a couple of times just out of curiosity. So, if you don't want to go full-bore but still enjoy it, you can set your own pace.

Lilla's point, and that of many who keep playing decade after decade, is not necessarily to sustain the same level of performance as when they were younger but to stay in the game. Make no mistake, though. These EALs are still competitive. I have seen many an 80-year-old beat out decades-younger athletes who did not have the same skill or confidence in adapting their strategy to course conditions.

The headline here for organizations is that long-time EALs can and want to stay competitive. They have irreplaceable value as the workforce expands to include three and four generations in many organizations. Rather than focusing on the inevitable changes that come with age, thriving organizations are tapping older EALs' depth of experience, robust relationships, and strategic and tactical insights to help them stay competitive. Agile organizations also spotlight the EALs who continue to learn and adapt and share their wisdom across generations to inspire all to do the same. The lesson here is not to overlook the ability of EALs like Lilla to stay agile and relevant. You may even be surprised by who crosses the finish line first!

Keep Moving

Lilla was understating when she shared that she didn't sit down much. She knows that to stay in the game, she must keep moving. When the snow isn't flying, Lilla stays agile and connected to Community by competing in tennis leagues, as well as hiking and kayaking. EALs in business have also learned that they can't sit still if they want to stay agile and relevant. T-Mobile is a great example because it has staked its reputation on its ability to do just this in a dynamic global market. It rewards leaders at all levels of the company who help it sustain its brand reputation and its results. Jon Freier, T-Mobile's executive vice president of retail channels, described one of the secrets of the company's success, sharing that "If there's a problem, they're going to tell you." You can't be agile and relevant without being in a constant state of listening and learning.

For T-Mobile, listening and learning means hosting a rolling series of employee meetings with company executives in New York and throughout the country. At these events, Freier and other leaders take in feedback and aim to respond with policy changes on the spot or with a decision within 24 hours. "That energizes the team," Freier says.

An agile and relevant workforce is vital to T-Mobile's competitiveness and its ability to beat rivals on customer service. For example, when the company conducted a nationwide hiring spree in 2017, it explicitly sought passionate and energetic job candidates. In the process, T-Mobile opened 1,500 stores, brought on 10,000 new employees, and saw revenue climb 8.3% to $40.6 billion.[2] Five years later, they, like their competitors, are shrinking their retail footprint in response to shifting consumer shopping habits and demands. Freier shared, "A one-size-fits-all approach to retail is long gone, and if we can't offer a multichannel, customized retail shopping experience, then we have missed the mark."[3] Staying agile and relevant is key to T-Mobile's success, measured by their record results[4] and by consistently ranking at the top of the "big three" carriers in customer satisfaction.[5]

Embodying an Agile Mindset

> I think mindset is probably a good 75% of almost anything you do. I think that is huge. You have the ability, but if you don't have the drive or the will to build on it, what good is the ability? I'm just going out to do it. Never quit.
>
> —Lilla Andrews, 82-year-old ski racer

The theme of agility and relevancy echoes across sectors led by EALs. For example, in the fashion industry, success depends on staying relevant to customers' ever-changing tastes. In practice, this means leading with an agile mindset that, once again, values listening, learning, and adapting over planning and control. Chris Mikulski, head of Human Resources, Americas at H&M, the EAL whom you met in Chapter 5, shared how he and his team embody an agile mindset, "We never get too comfortable with our strategies. We're agile and changing all the time, minute to minute. We set off on an idea, we test things, we measure outcomes, and when we see a big opportunity, we shift. We constantly shift."

Staying relevant to constantly changing conditions and to customer and stakeholder needs is the specialty of EALs. They know they cannot stay in the game if they have not kept up with the changing rules, players, and emerging technology and trends.

The imperative of continuous learning is amplified if you are exploring a new field or developing a new skill so you can adapt to the changes in your industry. The leaders who succeed over the long haul don't let the fear or anxiety that is part of any learning process hold them back. They assess the risks and rewards and persevere through the messy and humbling experience of learning new skills and knowledge on their way to developing competency and confidence. Humility is a critical element for agility. As soon as you lose it, you also lose a mindset open to new discoveries.

Staying Agile and Relevant in Your Meaningful Identity

You have seen how EALs discover and develop their Meaningful Identity through participating in and co-creating Community. You have also seen how the vibrant exchange of relational energy motivates the continuous learning of Competition and the ability to prioritize the Commitment necessary to stay in the game.

Such intentional engagement is a kind of learning agility dance. As we experiment with and practice new steps, we receive feedback and adapt in our quest to be relevant to ourselves, as well as to our dynamic present and emerging future. The variously attributed quote, "How can I know what I think until I see what I say?"[6] beautifully reflects this dance of relevancy. We learn what we are "saying" through each embodied feedback loop and adapt based on the responses. These adaptations become integrated into how we know ourselves and how others know us as our Meaningful Identity emerges and evolves.

Do What Scares You

No one understands what it feels like to learn new steps in an ever-changing dance more than James Hlavenka, Esq., whom you met in Chapter 5. You may remember that after years of building his career as a pharmaceutical legal counselor, Jim had the opportunity to make a radical shift—it would disrupt the role he traditionally played in the industry and how he was known to his colleagues. He knew that his core values of integrity, collaboration, and patient safety were unchanged and were, in fact, even more aligned with the new opportunity. Yet, there were significant risks to consider.

> I had to face a lot of fears. I had moved my whole family, my whole life, away from the Northeast and my network to come to UCB in Atlanta. When presented with this new opportunity, I sought advice and feedback from many, some of which worked to discourage me from taking on such a risk. "You're about to jump into something that's a pilot—not tried and true. If it fails, what are you going to do? You must know there may not be an immediate return ticket to your prior role."

Jim's decision required deep reflection and keen embodied awareness, even for someone who consistently practiced Embodied Agile Leadership. In addition to assessing the risks and potential rewards discussed in Chapter 3, Jim engaged with another significant risk: leaving the comfort of his well-planned career path and outwardly known Meaningful Identity. Jim was deeply attuned to his hard-won identity, respected reputation, and belongingness to a profession in which he played a clear and important role, and making the move carried both financial and emotional risks.

While the risks were daunting, ultimately, Jim decided to do what scared him and move forward. He recognized that his fear signaled the opportunity to grow as a leader and expand his impact. Jim (like other

EALs) knew that the most important person he needed to be relevant to was himself, as well as his values. This value-driven relevancy is the high-octane fuel for agility.

In many ways, Jim's internal dialogue leading up to the leap into the new role mirrored his industry's competing priorities and constraints. These tensions became clearer to him when eight months into the company's agile transformation, we worked together to create a high-engagement agile leadership off-site retreat. Until this role shift, Jim had spent his career counseling internal and external clients on risk management and ensuring the highest level of compliance with industry regulations and standards. Now he was charged with leading the effort to improve the company's speed, agility, and responsiveness to patient needs while maintaining that same level of integrity and compliance. Jim built trust and guided his division through an impactful transformation by leading with learning agility, curiosity, and collaboration.

Assessing and responding to each risk has proved worth the rewards for Jim, as well as for UCB and the patients they serve. The impact of the Agile transformation efforts within UCB was "measurable and striking." After 18 months of the transformation, the UCB business unit saw reduced errors and improved resource efficiency, including cutting the average development cycle by 26% and increasing market readiness by 25%. These results directly impact UCB's ability to stay relevant and responsive to patient needs.

The commitment and the shift to a way of working centered on learning and adaptation also positively impacted the UCB team. Regular pulse checks throughout the transformation process found the following: "Sustained increases in favorability scores across vectors contemplating ways of working and culture compared with historical data. Namely, the team self-reported a 90% favorability rating for collaboration and 88% favorability rating for satisfaction (a 38% increase over baseline), in addition to significant, sustained gains in favorability ratings for clarity in communication (76%) and timely decision-making (75%)."[7]

Complementing the measurable improvements, members of the cross-functional teams reported that they were learning from each other through their collaborations rather than simply updating each other from isolated silos. Along the way, team members taught each other about their functional areas and roles, which greatly enhanced mutual understanding and the ability to collaborate. The Agile transformation's impact has been felt well beyond the quality of collaboration; team members reported that "they are better equipped to ask each other questions and learn how to leverage each other's talents to create better solutions for the patients they serve."[8]

By choosing to do what scared him and learning and adapting with Embodied Agile Leadership, Jim continues to stay in the game and realize the rewards for himself, his family, his organization, and the patients they serve—a dynamic expression of his Meaningful Identity. Most recently, he has taken on the role of Head of Strategy and Operations, where he has the opportunity to proactively shape how the UCB Neurology business continues to bring value to patients. By practicing learning agility, Jim can anticipate challenges and shape opportunities, as well as draw on his experiences to communicate and collaborate with cross-functional colleagues across departments. All agile systems need boundary spanners like Jim who risk taking on new roles and leading for a dynamic future.

Across domains, EALs stay in the game by staying out of their comfort zone and doing what scares them. Like Lilla and Jim, they get restless if they spend too much time on their metaphorical couches. They need to get up and get moving. Get training. Get learning. Get going. Get changing. You will learn more about this in the next chapter and discover more ways EALs stay strong and resilient.

COACHING
Staying Agile and Relevant

This chapter's coaching questions will help you discover any additional shifts you can make to help you stay agile and relevant.

 Download the *Embodied Reflection and Action Journal* with all of the coaching prompts, as well as additional resources here: https://pamela-meyer.com/staying-in-the-game-resources/ or use the QR code on the left.

What? *Practicing Embodied Awareness and Assessment*	• What are you learning in response to your reflections and actions from prior iterations, so far? • What are you experiencing or aware of when you are being agile and relevant to yourself, your values, and the needs of your core stakeholders? • Inspired by the stories in this chapter, what opportunities come to mind for you to "keep moving" and "do what scares you"?
Gut? *Engaging Your Whole Person*	• What are you feeling (physically, emotionally, and otherwise) when you are being agile and relevant? When you are doing what scares you?
So What? *Making Sense and Prioritizing*	• How is staying agile and relevant important to your life today? • Which experiences of agility and relevancy are most engaging and energizing to you and most sustaining to your experience of livelihood? • If time or resources are constrained, which aspects of the experiences and practices you have described do you want to prioritize?
Now What? *Making Decisions and Acting*	• With your embodied experience of staying agile and relevant in mind, what shifts might you make to increase the possibility of it? • What obstacles are getting in the way of staying agile and relevant? • How can you, or who/what can you engage, to help remove these obstacles? • With these insights in mind, what actions can you take or activities do you want to prioritize, and invest in, to heighten and sustain your agility and relevancy (and the rewards that come with it)? • What new habits or practices will help you sustain your ability to stay agile and relevant?

CHAPTER 10

STAYING STRONG AND RESILIENT

That was not going to be my story.
—Desiree Adaway, business owner and change agent

The strength and resiliency exhibited by masters athletes and other embodied agile leaders (EALs) inspire me. I have worked and trained with EALs as they persevere through all conditions, adapting to new innovations and change, industry constraints, or personal limitations brought on by age, injury, or illness. Every day I learn more from these EALs who continue to compete at the top of their game with grace and good humor year after year.

There is no template for strength and resiliency in any given situation or for any individual person. Yet, we tend to assign these capacities to those who find a way to move forward, especially when confronted with life's greatest challenges. In telling the stories of some of these inspiring EALs, I have primarily focused on their successes. However, you may be surprised to know that without exception, the EALs who shared their stories with me have experienced a wide range of obstacles along the way. These have included physical, emotional, and financial setbacks, as well as the countless everyday challenges of life in the 21st century.

The setback, of course, is never the most interesting part of the story. The same is true in our lives and, yes, once again, in ski racing. A coach once helped me put a rough training run into perspective by describing slalom racing as "a series of linked recoveries." In this chapter, you will discover how EALs approach the "linked recoveries" of their lives and work. Specifically, how they engage their Community, renew their passion for Competition, and continue to prioritize the Commitment that enables them to make those recoveries and stay strong and resilient.

Embodying Strength

Embodied strength starts with embodied awareness. Becoming aware of the ways we are strong and engaging those strengths to adapt to new challenges and opportunities is a practice that has guided educators and coaches of EALs for decades.

Strength in every sport starts with the core. Every athlete knows no amount of talent or skill can compensate for a weak core. Physically, of course, this means building literal core strength, including the torso, abdominal, back, and hip muscles. Awareness and engagement of a strong physical core supports the good posture, balance, and stability we need to respond and adapt in a dynamic environment.

EALs in business must be equally aware of and intentional in developing their core strengths or competencies. Professors C.K. Prahalad and Gary Hamel wrote in their impactful *Harvard Business Review* article:

"[core competence] does not diminish with use. Unlike physical assets, which deteriorate over time, competencies are enhanced as they are applied and shared. But competencies still need to be nurtured and protected; knowledge fades if it is not used. Competencies are the glue that binds existing businesses. They are also the engine for new business development.[1]

Core competency in business also refers to the unique strengths and capabilities of an organization that sets it apart from its competitors. For example, it could be a unique technology, a proprietary process, a strong brand, or a high capacity to adapt to shifting customer needs. Just like a strong core in an athlete, core competencies in business provide a foundation for organizational success. They help a company to be resilient, maintain stability in the market, and grow. Businesses with a strong foundation of their core competencies can develop new products and services, generating new revenue streams. EALs drive this virtuous cycle of innovation, learning, and adaptation that reinforces their Meaningful Identity and fosters further engagement and growth.

Strength + Flexibility = Resiliency

Athletes who focus only on building strength are no more able to compete in sports that require speed and agility than companies that focus only on building a strong infrastructure without fostering Embodied Agile Leadership at all levels. Strength without flexibility is not strength at all.

If you are not agile, you are fragile.

The long list of big and "strong" brands that have met their demise because they could not adapt to changing consumer needs or adopt and integrate emerging technology is proof: If you are not agile, you are fragile. However, strength *with* flexibility enables resiliency, the ability to come back and "bounce forward" from disruptions and setbacks.

Embodying an Agile Mindset (Again)

Throughout the stories of EALs, you have seen the role that mindset plays in fostering and inspiring strength and resiliency. Product Group Manager and ski instructor Abbie More, whom you first met in Chapter 4, shared how she carries her agile mindset and mental toughness from her regular morning workouts into her workplace for strength and resiliency.

> Two of my workouts are circuit classes with ten stations set up, and we do five rounds. It's 30 seconds of work at each station and 30 seconds of rest. I have a friend who comes to these who's a retired state trooper. He will typically be at the station right next to me, so either I follow him or he follows me. Besides all the banter back and forth, it's funny because we'll get to a station, and maybe there's a burpee station or another tough station. Whatever the station is, he approaches it like, "Ugh, I gotta go do this one."
>
> I'm like, "Really? That's my favorite!" I remember one of the first times we did this. He'd get to each station and say, "Oh, I have to go to this station." I was like, "That's my

favorite!" All the way around. Suddenly he looked at me, and says, "I know what you're doing." I said, "You have to make each of them your favorite. You have to look at them as, 'I'm going to have fun here. I have to have fun for only 30 seconds, and I'm going to make the best of it.'"

Let's face it, do you really think burpees are fun? Nobody does, but if you tell yourself, "This is my favorite. I am going to have fun with it," then you can find something positive about it. It's the same with work. "Hey, I have a challenging issue ahead of me. It's stuff I really don't like dealing with. It's not sexy. It's not fun. But it's necessary. I'm going to make it my favorite, too.

The kind of intentional mindset shifting Abbie describes is the hallmark of EALs who can stay strong and resilient. Rather than give in to the first impulse to resist tough challenges or simply "get through them," EALs actively choose a positive mindset and find the opportunity within them. By doing so, they are finding and creating energy rather than becoming unnecessarily depleted. This is why people love working with (and working out next to) EALs! And who knows, maybe you will learn to love the burpees in your day, too.

Embodying Resiliency

The resiliency and remarkable comebacks of the EALs you have met are too many to do justice to here. While I've already mentioned several of the countless stories I've heard and comebacks I've witnessed, two have stayed with me and inspired me over the years. Sharing comeback stories ensures that we don't see only "the glory" without hearing more of "the story."

Slowing Down to Go Fast, Literally

By any measure, Lilla Andrews, whom you met in Chapter 9, is remarkable. She is still competing in alpine ski racing at a high level in her 80s and leading an active and engaged life year-round. From what I have shared so far, you might think she is one of those people who are particularly blessed with good health. But this is not the case. In reality, Lilla's ability to stay strong and resilient, especially in recent decades, has had everything to do with her intentionality.

Lilla had been actively competing for a decade at age 60 when, after experiencing "more neck and back pain than usual," doctors found a tumor growing in her spinal cord. The good news was that the tumor was benign. The bad news was that, given the tumor's location inside her spinal cord near the top of her spine, removing it caused serious nerve damage. Overnight, Lilla went from being able to race down the mountain at top speed and run her peers around the tennis court to needing to start completely over. "Not knowing where my feet were, spatially, it took me a couple of years to learn how to walk and ski again," she shared. To this day, Lilla continues to experience "numbness and a feeling of an electric current running through her legs, feet, and left arm 24/7." This would be unbearable for someone who leads a sedentary life, but for Lilla, whose game depends on a high degree of embodied awareness, it was a call to action.

Someone with a less developed Meaningful Identity, a less robust Community, or less love of the challenge of Competition might have abandoned the Commitment to stay in the game. Just the opposite happened for Lilla. She shared that the setback only reinforced and even created a new urgency for her. "I remember being driven to do all that I could *when* I could. Because I never knew when I wouldn't be able to do anything." It's this intentionality that has youngsters in their 60s telling Lilla that they want to be like her when they grow up.

> "I remember being driven to do all that I could *when* I could. Because I never knew when I wouldn't be able to do anything."

The stories of Lilla and many EALs who demonstrate their strength and resiliency inspire us. They remind us when we wake up with a few real or imagined maladies and are tempted to bail on our plans for the day to realistically assess and adapt if necessary, but by all means to "keep going."

Holding Identity Lightly

Setbacks are humbling. And disruptive. They can challenge our very sense of who we are and make us doubt ourselves and our purpose. EALs are not immune from these challenges. Rather, they experience them deeply and with their whole selves and bodies. They must experience deeply if they are to find the restorative energy that lies within.

Desiree Adaway, the EAL whom you first met in Chapter 4 as she met her moment with her Meaningful Identity by launching her new business, shared how her early experience and guiding philosophy help her stay resilient.

I always say, "Nothing lasts forever." Nothing good, nothing bad. Even when it's great. Even when it's horrible, there is this sense for me that I ride the wave. Sometimes it's big and takes me far, and sometimes it will work me.

The fear of all the possible "what ifs" described in Chapter 3 holds many people back from even sticking their big toe in the water, let alone catching a wave. These fears can keep us from getting in the game in the first place, let alone getting *back* into the game after a setback.

We are freer to play when we hold our identity lightly, including what other people think of us, or any status or credentials we may have achieved, or other trappings of success we have enjoyed. Desiree learned this long before I did.

> You can always start over. I was never tied to a title or this image…this very classist elitist idea of degree or titles. I believe any work is of value, and there is no shame in it. I used to tease a friend, "is this the summer we serve ice cream?" Even though I have a great business and make great money. But I still have the mindset of "So what if I do?" There is no shame in selling ice cream. I don't have my ego tied to what I do. I'm not afraid. I've had my car repossessed. And guess what? I woke up the next day.

Setbacks and disruptions are unique opportunities for reflection and finding meaning and renewed strength. They are also opportunities for your Community to hold and support you—and for you to let them. Doing so can take courage and humility.

The car was repossessed as part of a year and a half when I was laid off and I couldn't find work. I have to tell you, I did so much internal work during that time. What am I really wanting? How am I showing up? What does my family need right now? What do I need? What are my non-negotiables? I have to tell you, I just surrendered more and more into this sense of gratitude. The days were rough. I remember getting into bed and thinking, "You know what? Today you had everything you needed. Your girls were good. Your house is here and good and fine. You had food. You had everything you needed today, and I'm going to be thankful in that moment."

The more difficult it became, the more and more I surrendered into this place of gratitude for what I did have and an understanding that this was a *moment* in my life, *not* my life. This was not my whole story. I said to myself, "My story is not one of failure. My story is one of victory."

It's difficult, right? But my best friend and other people helped me get through that time. My sister bought me groceries, and my best friend, Pam, said, "What size do the girls wear? I'm buying their school uniforms for the year," or whatever. So many people supported me. Cared for me and cared about me. I just said to myself over and over again, "This is one moment in your life. This is not your life. Your story is one of victory."

I have two children now—and I see them doing some of the same things. They take those risks. I have to step back sometimes and let them do it. I always tell them, "You can recover. It doesn't matter what it is. You can recover. And if you can't, that will be okay, too. You can handle it."

Desiree continues to stay strong and resilient with her agile mindset and deep Community engagement. Years after first meeting her and being inspired by how seriously she took herself and her game, I had the opportunity to experience the power of her work firsthand. When our program at DePaul University was going through a significant disruptive change, Desiree led a diverse group of my learning colleagues through a transformative workshop in which we reflected on how our various identities impacted our co-created learning environments.

Resiliency Through Hardiness and Compassion

With Desiree's guidance, my colleagues and I discovered what researchers identified as the two most consistent traits of resiliency in athletes coming back from injury: hardiness and compassion.[2,3] A constellation of attitudes, beliefs, and behaviors, hardiness is similar to grit, introduced earlier. Hardy people can weather storms that can keep others in their shelters long after the sun has returned. However, hardiness alone is not enough for resiliency season after season. For this, we need compassion, for ourselves and others. Mental skills coach Carrie Cheadle and fitness writer Cindy Kuzma describe compassion in terms of generosity, or "the willingness to extend grace to yourself and others."[4]

Through especially challenging times, we need to lean into our capacities for both hardiness and compassion to find renewal because adversity can trigger our harsher impulses toward ourselves or others.

Harshness is not hardy; it is destructive. In these times when we might be tempted to be reactive, or shut down and motor through, we need to slow down and extend a bit of grace to ourselves and others. Grace allows us the space to feel our feelings from outrage to despair and everything in between. In grace we can also find new space for hope, healing, and connection.

Few times have been more challenging in recent years as the pandemic and the killing of George Floyd by Minneapolis police officers. Demonstrating a robust mix of hardiness and compassion, Desiree and her colleagues developed and delivered important thought and action-provoking virtual learning programs and consultancies. While many individuals and organizations who responded to these events in the immediate aftermath quickly returned to the comfort of business as usual, Desiree's work has only deepened and expanded. EALs stay strong and resilient, guided by a true passion, within a generative Community. When EALs, such as Desiree, meet their moment with such Commitment and purpose, they inspire the rest of us to meet ours.

A Staying in the Game Workout

Each week on the popular show *The Wide World of Sports*, Jim McKay narrated "the thrill of victory and the agony of defeat."[5] This famous phrase is seared into the memory banks of generations of sports fans. We are enthralled by "the human drama of athletic competition," and McKay and his team brought it to us from all corners of the globe for decades. The reason athletic competition is a favorite source of inspiration and guidance well beyond any specific field of play is because of its inherent drama.

Of course, athletes don't just show up on the day of the competition, relying on their innate talent and high hopes. They spend countless hours off the field intentionally preparing so they can be strong and resilient while playing. Working with EALs whose livelihoods depend on staying in the game gives me a front-row seat to their development needs and critical success factors. With rare exceptions, those who consistently play at the top of their game set themselves up for success by preparing, training, seeking out coaching and feedback, and also making time for resting, recovering, and renewing.

Prepare

A bit different than planning, preparing is about getting to a state of readiness. Preparing starts with getting into the mindset and Meaningful Identity of an EAL. Your mindset and Meaningful Identity propel other aspects of preparing, which may include mapping out coaching, training schedules, and other logistics. For example, by late summer my 70+-year-old racing friends have already scoped out the pass deals and senior discounts and made their purchases. In the fall, when the race schedules come out, Lilla and other masters map out their schedules, travel plans, and accommodations; set aside needed funds; and prepare their equipment, and, of course, their bodies.

I have shared several ways that EALs in business prepare to play. They also begin by engaging a positive agile mindset. EALs embrace this mindset wholeheartedly, and often do it in Community. For example, EALs at Umqua Bank, a community bank based in Portland, Oregon, whose innovative practices I profiled in *The Agility Shift*,[6] start each day by convening their entire staff at each location for a "Motivational Moment." In just a few short minutes, Umpqua EALs may lead their colleagues in anything from a playful improv game, group sing-along, or even a rousing game of marshmallow dodgeball. While some might dismiss this preparation as frivolous, it has had a serious impact. An upbeat tone and agile mindset are engaged, Community connections are fostered, and relational energy is generated in a way that carries over to the rest of the day's interactions. This kind of intentional preparation allows you to hold your plans lightly and adjust as needed. With a mindset of anxious confidence, you know that you have done all you can to prepare for the game while expecting the inevitable unexpected.

Another excellent practice for preparing for the dynamic future is to raise awareness of your and your teams' core strengths. EALs do this by engaging their colleagues in activities that embody their vision, mission, and values, as well as their strategic priorities. These range from community volunteer projects to lively strategic engagement sessions. Such activities also help create alignment and Commitment, as well as highlight strengths and identify opportunities for more learning and development. Speaking of which . . .

Train

As I discovered early on in my return to ski racing, no amount of hubris, or even innate talent, can overcome a lack of training. Staying in the game requires getting and staying fit all year on dry land and seeking out as much time training in actual race conditions. In addition to staying active and engaged year-round, Karl, Toshio, Max, Lilla, and many other regulars are out on the race hill most weeks for training sessions. They wouldn't dream of competing without having done so.

As an EAL, your training will be as varied as the games you play. Most EALs must continue training to lead in an increasingly uncertain world. In addition, perhaps you are training to support the success of integrating your business with another, expanding to global markets, or leading your digital transformation. Or perhaps you are training to be a more agile team member. Along with any of this training, you may well be training to expand your ability to lead in a way that embodies your values and makes room for you to thrive in your whole life, not just your business life. Any combination of these prospects, and countless others, can only be realized with intentional learning and growth. Identifying your best resources for this learning and finding supportive spaces to experiment with new ways of thinking, being, and leading are critical to your success.

It may not be so important *how* you train as *that* you train.

It may not be so important *how* you train as *that* you train. Fitness trainers report that those who stay with their Commitment to their goals do so through a combination of consistency and variety. That means that they consistently prioritize health and fitness but do so in a variety of ways so that they don't get bored. Variety also ensures that new learning sticks. Our brains and bodies love novelty. For example, off-site retreats and intensive training sessions are fantastic novel immersion opportunities, but don't overlook the potential novelty of short virtual courses, videos, podcasts, books, and articles. These training options deepen and become "stickier" when experimented with and shared in Community. For example, I have participated in regular journal and book discussion groups in organizations with participants invited to share and discuss fresh ideas and perspectives. For maximum impact, consider using the *Embodied Reflection and Action Framework* to reflect on and record your insights during or after each of your training and learning experiences.

Seek Out Coaching and Integrate Feedback

Training alone without coaching and feedback can simply give you more time to repeat and ingrain bad habits. Often, at the bottom of a training run, I meet up with a coach or fellow racer and hear just the right feedback to help me progress. For example, a seasoned racer recently asked me, "Do you know you tend to be late on your right-footed turns?" Because I was repeating a familiar pattern, I was *not* aware. This simple question gave me just the focus I needed to help break an old habit. Coaching is a great way to increase your embodied awareness, which is the first step toward disrupting ingrained habits.

EALs in the workplace don't often have the luxury of video reviews but can still ask for real-time feedback. Be sure to be as specific as possible in your request. For example, as you head into a meeting, you might tell a trusted colleague or even your entire team what you are working on, such as, "I'm working on making room for everyone to be heard and not dominating the conversation. Can I ask for your help by letting me know if you see improvements and what I still need to work on?" Such feedback can be hard to ask for and sometimes be even harder to hear. Our reptilian brains tend to favor feedback that bolsters our self-esteem and reinforces our positive self-image. Fortunately, many seasoned coaches are experts at supporting your Meaningful Identity while helping you meet your goals of continuous improvement and growth.

Be Specific

One of my race coaches encourages training specificity as each racer slips into the start gate. He'll ask, "What are you working on this run?" When his racer responds, "Making faster transitions into the next turn," he'll reply, "So how are you going to do that?" This exchange might go a few rounds until both are satisfied that the racer has a clear and actionable focus for the next run.

You can hold yourself to this same standard of specificity with a few follow-up reflections or questions in the "Now What?" phase of your *Embodied Reflection and Action Framework*. For example, if you find yourself with a "Now What?" of "Become more consistent modeling and sharing my learning with my team," you can ask, "And how am I going to do that?" until you have a clear and actionable insight that you can experiment with on *your* next "run."

Rest, Recover, and Renew

No one can engage in Competition, whether motivated by intrinsic or extrinsic rewards, without prioritizing rest and recovery. Professional ski racers have a name for this time at the end of the season; they call it "Fat April." Named for the month that follows the last race on the World Cup schedule, "Fat April" is when athletes allow themselves to take a break from their rigorous training and competition schedule and maybe even indulge in a few treats that are not on their nutrition plan.

EALs recognize that, despite the mechanistic model that first inspired traditional organizational structures and organized the work within them, people are not machines. Prioritizing longer breaks from the intensity of Competition is not reserved for elite athletes and others who can manage the time and resources to step away. The burnout and turnover rates of top talent in organizations indicate that many feel pushed to the brink by the demands of companies that continue to drive them as if they were merely mechanical pieces of equipment.

> Many of us hide our personal lives (or that we even have personal lives) at work for fear of being seen as not devoted to the job 24/7. We answer emails and take conference calls in the middle of the night. We come to work ill.[7]
> —Desiree Adaway, business owner and change agent

All of us know that shorter bursts of extraordinary effort can be required to respond to time-sensitive challenges and emergencies. We also know that such fire drills aren't sustainable for doing business long term and, more importantly, don't work. Athletes and EALs know that they perform at their best and can continue to learn and improve only by showing up each day feeling their best. And best starts with prioritizing sustainable ways of working that are more likely to energize than to deplete.

EALs also check in with themselves and their teams to discern whether they need to prioritize rest, recovery, or renewal. This self-awareness is the *embodied* part of Embodied Agile Leadership. The first question, then, is not "How am I doing?" It is "How am I *feeling*?" New innovations in wearable technology help athletes track their daily exertion and recovery and help them modify their training plan accordingly. However, you don't need to invest in yet another gadget to tune into your own embodied experience to make similar modifications in your life and work.

Tuning into your embodied state will help you discern if you need to prioritize rest, recovery, renewal, or a combination of all three. For example, if your answer to "What am I feeling?" is "I didn't sleep well the last few nights and am not feeling as sharp as I would like," then you need to prioritize *rest* however you can. A depleted state is also not likely to be your best day to initiate a new project, convene your team for brainstorming, or engage in a difficult conversation. If you are experiencing a setback, illness, or injury, prioritizing *recovery* is in order. Big efforts, stressful projects, or other high-intensity endeavors call for *renewal*, as do leaders, teams, and entire organizations that recognize the need to renew their vision, values, and culture to be more competitive in a dynamic future.

Even in a climate when it is becoming more acceptable to talk about and seek support for mental health, prioritizing your well-being can be disruptive. It can disrupt your schedule and plans and those of others who care about, depend on, and collaborate with you. Prioritizing your well-being can be especially disruptive to your identity and how you see yourself and believe you are known in the world. EALs seek out support, so the possibility of such disruptions does not become an obstacle to recovery. Organizations that value sustainable well-being also create access to and widely communicate the available resources for regaining and sustaining well-being, as well as support everyone who takes advantage of them.

Generous Strength and Resiliency

The common thread through each of the stories and practices described here is generosity. We cannot be leaders who co-create environments where our colleagues thrive without fostering a climate of generosity, starting with ourselves. Western culture has celebrated those who forge ahead despite all costs, even to themselves. Forging ahead without nourishment is stingy, not generous. Such behavior may achieve short-term results but is not sustainable in the long run. Staying in the game, and staying strong and resilient, requires generosity and compassion for ourselves and others as we build on each others' strengths and prioritize sustainable practices that enable resiliency.

COACHING
Staying Strong and Resilient

This chapter's coaching questions are a wonderful opportunity to practice being generous and compassionate with yourself. By giving yourself a few minutes to reflect on the insights and lessons you learned from this chapter, you will recognize your wealth of strength and resiliency capabilities and identify opportunities to share it with others.

Download the *Embodied Reflection and Action Journal* with all of the coaching prompts, as well as additional resources here: https://pamela-meyer.com/staying-in-the-game-resources/ or use the QR code on the left.

What? *Practicing Awareness and Assessment*	• What are you learning in response to your reflections and actions, so far? • What are you experiencing or aware of when you are being strong and resilient. • Inspired by the stories and practices in this chapter, what opportunities come to mind for you to lead with an agile mindset and stay strong and resilient, and help others do the same?
Gut? *Engaging Your Whole Person*	• What are you feeling (physically, emotionally, and otherwise) when you are being strong and resilient?
So What? *Making Sense and Prioritizing*	• How are strength and resiliency important to your life today? • Which experiences of strength and resiliency are most engaging and energizing to you? Which most sustain your experience of livelihood? • If time or resources are constrained, which aspects of the experiences and practices you have described do you want to prioritize?
Now What? *Making Decisions and Acting*	• With your embodied experience of staying strong and resilient in mind, what shifts might you make to more consistently and compassionately enjoy them? How might you help others recognize and build their strengths and capacity for resiliency? • What obstacles are getting in the way of staying strong and resilient? • How can you or who/what can you engage to help remove these obstacles? • With these insights in mind, what actions can you take or activities do you want to prioritize, and invest in, to heighten and sustain your strength and resiliency and the rewards that come with it? • What new habits or practices will help you sustain your and others' ability to stay strong and resilient?

CHAPTER 11

STAYING HAPPY

When I load the chair lift with three young girls, all racers from Stowe, Vermont, I have no idea I'm about to be treated to a lesson in happiness. Once settled in, the girls quickly strike up a conversation. The first asks me my name, and when I tell her, she immediately finds a point of connection—her best friend's mom's name, Camela, rhymes with mine. Slightly rattled that I am in the mom category, I am slow to follow up. Undeterred, they each introduce themselves, starting with "I'm Esther!" followed by, "My name is North!" and, "I'm Kikki!" exclaims the girl next to me who had started the ball rolling. "Those are great ski racer names!" I respond.

After a quick chat about our race camps and with only a few minutes left in the ride, Esther shouts, "I have an idea! I'll start a rhythm, and then you all add something to it!" She starts her beat, and Kiki quickly jumps in with an alternating beat, then I add a vocal "boop." North then clinks her ski poles together complementing the rhythm we have created. We keep our little jam session going until it's time to raise the lift bar and prepare to unload. As we all slide down the unloading ramp, North exclaims, "We sounded pretty good!

That was fun!" We all chorus, "Have a great day!" and ski off in our separate directions.

These few minutes of chairlift improv and unbridled joy stayed with me the entire day. In fact, they have stayed with me for years. The experience stands out because it was so wonderfully unexpected and included many of the ingredients we often associate with happiness: being in the present moment, enjoying the camaraderie of friends, welcoming the stranger, being curious, and being playful. As someone who has spent decades helping adults reclaim this natural ability to be agile and improvise, I was delightfully humbled at my chairlift friends' enthusiastic practice of one of the central tenants of improv, saying "yes, and . . ." In our short ride together, there was no time to argue about what game we would play or what rules we would play by. As soon as Esther made her suggestion, the rest immediately agreed and built on it, leaving no one out, including the new "mom-ish" woman.

While tempting, I don't want to dissect this experience any further. My embodied experience of energy, connectedness, and lightness is enough to tell me that I was happy. Perhaps even joyful. I could appreciate this delightful experience even more thanks to a dinner conversation I had years earlier . . .

Are You Happy?

Sometimes a seemingly casual conversation can impact your life. That happened for me one night at dinner with my doctoral program professor, Peter Park. A leader in participatory action research, Peter articulated and promoted the value of interactive and relational knowledge in human and organizational development.[1] His belief in the importance of creating space for knowledge and action by people on the margins of power grew out of his work facilitating and collaborating on social change projects worldwide. Peter invited me to grab a bite at a nearby café after a graduate seminar he led because he was curious to hear more about my research on the spaces adults create to play with new ideas. However, I knew the real opportunity was for me to learn more about *his* experience doing just this across cultures.

At dinner, he shared his own early lived experiences of play. Growing up in Korea, he remembered hours playing made-up games with his friends and kicking the soccer ball around the playground at the Catholic school he attended. Then one day, something changed. One of the nuns had noticed Peter, an introvert by nature, sitting by himself at lunch. She sat beside him and asked, "Are you happy, Peter?" Up until that point, he shared that he had never really thought about it one way or another. He was simply living his life as a young boy, much like the young racers I encountered on the chairlift years later. But, of course, now he couldn't help but reflect on whether or not he was happy. Over the years, Peter shared, he had realized he was never as happy as he had been before the nun asked him the question.

Through his story, Peter warned to be careful of putting such ephemeral, personal lived experiences under the microscope lest we dispel their magic. With Peter's caution as my guide, my intention in what follows is to *describe* rather than *prescribe* some of the dimensions of happiness as they relate to staying in the game. In this chapter, I invite you to not so much ponder the question "am I happy?" as pay attention to the aspects of your work and life that give you joy, energy, and an overall experience of being well. Once again, I will share a few stories to help spur your imagination.

Being Happy Vs. Doing Happy

Happiness is booming. Or, at least, interest in what makes us happy is. Countless books, podcasts, documentaries, and articles confirm what your parents and grandparents always told you. Money can't buy happiness. Now let's not kid ourselves that money is irrelevant. It can buy you time, which can create more opportunities to create the meaningful connections and build Community that are the fabric of a fuller life. Money can also help give you more freedom to engage in the continuous learning of Competition and to prioritize the Commitments that enable you to stay in the game.

However, research shows that once these fundamental needs are met, those with significantly more resources don't turn out to be significantly happier.[2] As you have seen by the many examples I have shared, and likely from your own experience, Embodied Agile Leaders (EALs) embody this wisdom in all their endeavors. Their motivation for staying in the game is guided much more by the enduring intrinsic rewards than by the often-fleeting external achievements. Intrinsic happiness is what Peter was experiencing before the nun's interrogation. He was simply being happy. The questioning created an unfamiliar self-consciousness rather than the embodied self-awareness that can spark an exploration of new possibilities.

Embodied self-awareness, and the insights and choices it can surface, is not the same as trying to "do" happiness based on someone else's idea of a good time. If you have ever been corralled to a corporate costume party or game day, you may have found yourself on one side or another of the fine line between the forced fun of "doing" happiness and the inviting playspace of "being" happy. The difference between doing and being is not so much in the outer appearances, but in your (and the organizers', if there are any) relationship to the shared space. When people become attached to having a specific experience, such as the nun's question implied, the likelihood of that experience happening organically is diminished. However, creating space for spontaneous connections and playfulness to emerge can provide just the permission for all forms of happiness to thrive.

Embodying Happiness

To walk the fine line between a prescriptive approach to happiness and a descriptive one, it may be helpful to understand happiness through another lens. This chapter's opening story of spontaneous play is an example of what is sometimes called hedonic happiness, which is pleasurable and often fleeting. For example, the fleeting happiness of the moment that might come with such experiences as standing at the top of the podium or exceeding your quarterly revenue goals could be characterized as hedonic. These are, by their very nature, temporal and soon fade with the glow of the spotlight or when eclipsed by the shadow of a tough setback or other challenges. The kind of happiness that most EALs value is the more enduring experience of overall "eudaimonic happiness" that is associated with an overall sense of being well.[3] This is the happiness that comes with embodying a Meaningful Identity and finding and staying in the game that gives you purpose and pleasure and an opportunity for play and passion.

Both types of happiness are important, and the Embodied Agile Leadership approaches I describe here help EALs stay happy to ensure they don't miss those unexpected opportunities to experience joy while prioritizing their overall experience of well-being. Staying happy, then, may not be so much the goal but the outcome of intentionally prioritizing and making space to inhabit your life fully. Once again, intentionality is key. We all know there is no way to avoid challenges and setbacks. For EALs, such challenges help them appreciate their happiness even more. They choose to hedge their bets with an agile mindset that focuses on the things within their span of control or influence. For EALs, this means they keep connecting, keep learning, and keep (re)prioritizing.

Keep Connecting

> I hang around young people. Helps keep you thinking forward all the time. I'm just gonna ski and get through it.
> It's just one season at a time.
> —Phil Capy, 87-year-old ski patroller

> It's a team thing. Of course, you want to do well for the team. You're with people 30 years younger, and they don't care. I don't think we put ages on each other. You're just a person or a friend or a skier, and it doesn't really matter what your age difference is.
> —Lilla Andrews, 82-year-old alpine ski racer

One of the oldest participants in my annual race camp is Paul. At age 84, he is still going strong and trains in conditions that can send people half his age back to the lodge. I asked him what motivated him to keep going when so many friends had moved to Florida or passed away. He replied, "Well, for starters, I don't like Florida. And I've always been active. I work out at the Y three times a week (except for during COVID). And my daughter, who lives near me, keeps me active. She'll come over and say, 'let's go for a bike ride!' and take me out and almost destroy me on a 30-mile ride."

But Paul doesn't sit around waiting for his daughter to keep him going, and she was certainly nowhere in sight on the windy, icy slope that day. Paul had driven to Colorado from New York with his 82-year-old friend Jimmy. When I asked Paul to tell me more about how he keeps going, it is not just what he said, but how he said it that has stayed with me.

> All of my best friends are dead. So when you lose your friends, you've got to replace them. You've got to make new friends. So I do things like volunteer. I volunteer to help with the gardening at our club. That's not something you do alone. They always assign you to work with someone, so I make new friends that way.

There was no self-pity or resignation in Paul's response. Neither was there a hardened callousness. Paul had simply assessed his current reality and found a way to keep connecting and, by connecting, to keep moving.

Paul's approach would come as no surprise to researchers Robert Waldinger, MD, and Marc Schulz, PhD, who are director and associate director of the generations-long Harvard Study of Adult Development.[4] They are in a unique position to report on the difference between what people *think* will make them happy early in their lives and what *actually* makes them happy when they reflect on their lives in their final years. In reviewing the data from study participants from early adulthood through all stages of life, they found some surprising and not-so-surprising insights. In early adult life, research participants perhaps understandably had their sights set on careers, accumulation of wealth, and status, assuming this is the foundation for happiness. Near the end of their lives, across socioeconomic lines, those who reported overall satisfaction with their lives were not those who achieved the most wealth, status, or *stuff*. It turns out the happiest lives were (and are) the most connected lives.[5]

The most connected lives are also the healthiest lives. In addition to the EALs' accounts of the importance of Community and the research I shared in Chapter 6, public health researchers have discovered that loneliness can increase the risk of death as much as smoking, obesity, or physical inactivity.[6] Fortunately, connectedness can avert this scenario.

Restoration Through Relationships

The Harvard study headline that those who cultivated and maintained meaningful relationships reported an overall sense of happiness in their lives, while people who did not deeply regretted that they did not sustain such connections, includes some additional hopeful news: It is never too late to build those relationships! One great way to start or enhance your meaningful connections is to follow study directors Waldinger and Schulz's suggestions. Begin by mapping your relationships on a matrix from energizing to depleting and from infrequent to frequent.[7] For a fuller picture, consider adding your significant activities and communities to your map on the Relational Web graphic on the next page.

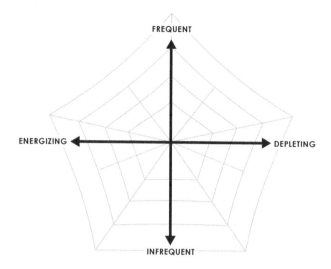

Mapping your relationships, communities, and activities is also an excellent way to assess your current reality. It helps to think about your embodied experience when you are engaged with the individuals, Communities, and activities on your map. Note which experiences energize you, pique your curiosity, and give you the feeling of being seen and of belonging. Which experiences deplete you, numb your curiosity, and leave you feeling more isolated rather than more connected and optimistic?

With this embodied awareness as the starting point, you can intentionally shift your energy away from those who are not supporting your Meaningful Identity or contributing to your happiness and toward those who do. Your new awareness and assessment is an opportunity for action. You can now more thoughtfully prioritize or perhaps reengage with those who give you energy and with whom you would like to spend more time.

Reflecting on the current reality of your meaningful relationships and the strength and diversity of your Relational Web is not a one-and-done proposition. EALs are constantly connecting. They, including Paul, know that you cannot simply establish a core group of friends, family, or co-workers and assume you are set for the foreseeable future. EALs nurture energizing relationships and consciously foster new ones for a dynamic future. These relationships and the experience of Community they provide, in turn, fuel and are fueled by the continuous learning of Competition, and as you have seen, help sustain your Commitment to staying in the game.

Keep Learning

When legendary theater director Peter Brook passed away at age 97, he was called "the greatest innovator of his generation" in *The New York Times*.[8] With "relentless curiosity," he never stopped learning and exploring, staging almost 100 productions across genres, beginning with a four-hour production of Hamlet in his toy theater at age 7. For Brook, staying in the game meant to "never stop asking questions." This quest continued through to his final production, aptly titled, "Why?" which opened in the fall of 2019, just months before the COVID-19 shut-down and less than two years before his death.

Brook's "relentless curiosity" is one I see in action on every race hill and in every workplace where EALs are thriving. The quest for learning and improvement is not a sideshow to the main event; it IS the main event. No matter how long EALs have been in the game or how many goals they have achieved, they continue asking the questions that fuel their quest.

This quest for improvement is at the heart of how EALs engage in Competition. When I met Lilla, this was the first thing that caught my attention after witnessing her glide beautifully through the course. On each chairlift ride we shared, she reflected on her last run and discussed possible new tactics as we viewed the course from above. When I caught up with Lilla mid-season to learn more about her motivation, she shared,

> I'm always trying to figure out what I'm doing and what I can do better to get a sharper edge. Even free skiing, for all these years, I've always been working on technique or how I feel I'm doing. And that's just been part of me. So after 35 years, I'm still trying to get it.

Like Peter Brook and Lilla, EALs staying engaged across domains are all doing so with "relentless curiosity." The quest and the questions it spurs are intimately entwined with their Meaningful Identity. With a dynamic future in mind, the opportunity for continued exploration is limitless.

Neuroscientists have found an embodied dimension to this quest. When we experience ourselves developing new skills and knowledge or discovering and demonstrating new talent, the hypothalamus in the brain rewards us with a dose of dopamine, sometimes called "the happiness hormone" because of how it makes us feel. Specifically, researchers found that "Changing dopamine [levels] immediately altered willingness to work and reinforced preceding action choices."[9] In other words, the positive embodied experience of new learning motivates us to continue the quest.

Keep (Re)Prioritizing

The most striking headline from my years-long inquiry into the "what," "why," and "how" of Embodied Agile Leadership is that all the dynamics of staying in the game, including our Meaningful Identity, are just that—dynamic. EALs don't expect them to be anything but.

The dynamic nature of the game means that we cannot become overly attached to one specific game or play our game in a specific way. There are just too many variables that are beyond our span of influence to give us even an illusion of control. This is why an agile mindset of learning and adapting runs through each of the dynamics of Embodied Agile Leadership.

High Participation, Low Attachment

Many of my early lessons in agility came from players in the theater who create entire evenings of entertainment based on one or two suggestions from the audience. These improvisers know they cannot control anything that happens on stage or in the audience; they can only control their response to each of the unexpected "gifts" they receive. To do this, they practice "high participation and low attachment." It might seem counterintuitive, but it is because improvisers can't control what happens next that they can enthusiastically commit to the present moment and all the discoveries they make there. For example, suppose one player gives the gift of a bouquet of flowers through high participation. In that case, the receiving player might discover it contains a sophisticated listening device. Then, with low attachment, the bouquet-giver, rather than pursuing her original intention of a Mother's Day scene, builds on the new "gift" by sharing the espionage mission she has received from headquarters. Both high participation and low attachment are necessary for the players to continue co-creating and moving the scene forward.

The same degree of high participation and low attachment is necessary to keep reprioritizing to co-create our unfolding lives and business opportunities. If we are overly attached to a specific understanding or perception of reality (e.g., what the bouquet of flowers means), we will not be able to adapt and stay in the game.

Businesses must constantly reprioritize based on their current reality, as well. Most new ventures are launched when the founders know the least about their new product or service's potential, let alone how it will respond to the needs of their customers. For example, without reprioritization, YouTube would never have become a billion-dollar video-sharing platform. The founders launched it as a dating site where people could post videos of themselves talking about what they seek in an ideal partner. They soon discovered that the Internet wasn't interested and quickly reprioritized to meet users' needs by opening the site up to any kind of video.[10] Reprioritizing for customer and stakeholder happiness created untold opportunity for more to play.

EALs who can keep reprioritizing stay in sync with and engaged in the generative energy of the game and the source of much happiness. For some, this means taking on a new role within the Community where they have enjoyed so much Competition and Commitment. For example, when one of the leaders in our local ski racing league experienced a health setback that kept him from competing, he continued to serve on the race committee, helped with registration, and even used his considerable skills to photograph our races.

While Art Clay, at age 85, and Ben Findley, age 84, the founders of the National Brotherhood of Skiers, don't ski anymore, they robustly joined in the celebration when NBS gathered in Vail in February 2023 to celebrate the 50th anniversary of the thriving organization. The celebration was themed "Soul on Snow" and drew over 2,000 participants. The success of NBS over the years in building Community and fostering lively Competition and Commitment is a testament to the founders' Embodied Agile Leadership, as is their ability to keep reprioritizing for a dynamic future. Art told *The New York Times,* "I've been doing this for so long, I used to say, 'Everyone raise your hand, so I can see you,' and now I say, 'Raise your cane!'" He reflected, "We might be older and not able to ski anymore, but it makes us real proud to see all these people out here."[11]

These EALs slow down enough to pay attention to the people and experiences that provide them with the most significant relational energy and opportunity to experience and express their Meaningful Identity. When they do, they discover that sometimes staying in the game means shifting the role they play within the Community; at other times, it may mean finding altogether new opportunities for engaging and expressing their Meaningful Identity.

EALs continually prioritize and reprioritize their Commitments based on their assessment of the current reality. Just as Peter Brook never stopped questioning and questing for the truth through theater and film, and Lilla continues her quest for the perfect edge angle, EALs keep connecting, keep learning, keep re-prioritizing, and of course, keep playing, to stay happy.

COACHING
Staying Happy

Without being prescriptive, this chapter's coaching questions can help you become more aware of the experiences and elements that contribute to your happiness and enable you to prioritize them.

 Download the *Embodied Reflection and Action Journal* with all of the coaching prompts, as well as additional resources here: https://pamela-meyer.com/staying-in-the-game-resources/ or use the QR code on the left.

What? *Practicing Embodied Awareness and Assessment*	• What am I learning in response to my reflections, experiments, and actions so far? • What do you notice when you experience moments of hedonic happiness? With which people, and in what places and activities are you more likely to experience it? • What contributes to your embodied experience of eudaimonic happiness?
Gut? *Engaging Your Whole Person*	• What are you feeling (physically, emotionally, and otherwise) when experiencing happiness? • What more does your body tell you about the value of happiness?
So What? *Making Sense and Prioritizing*	• How is the experience of happiness that you have just described relevant to your current life and values? • How does staying happy fit into or influence your whole life?
Now What? *Making Decisions and Acting*	• With your embodied experience of happiness in mind, what shifts might you make to increase the possibility of it? • What obstacles are getting in the way of staying happy? • How can you or who/what can you engage to help remove these obstacles? • What actions can you take or activities do you want to prioritize, and invest in, to heighten and sustain your happiness and the rewards that come with it? • What new habits or practices will help you sustain your happiness?

CHAPTER 12

A SPECIAL NOTE TO THE C-SUITE

Leading and Learning with Agility for a Dynamic Future

If you have read this far, I hope you have found several themes and practices to help you find, get in, and stay in your game. I've highlighted stories and lessons of individual Embodied Agile Leaders (EALs) wherever they find themselves—on the side of a mountain or inside a boardroom, operating room, or lunchroom. This focus is driven by the understanding that an *EAL is anyone who spots a challenge or opportunity and embodies an agile and effective response.*

However, because much of my work in organizations across industries is with C-suite leaders or those who report directly to them, I now want to shift focus. Keep reading if you currently occupy what is sometimes called the C-suite, aspire to or have influence with these leaders, or engage with colleagues who do.

"You know who *really* needs to be here..."

I've lost count of the number of people who have raised their hands during one of my leadership development sessions and shared, "What we are learning and doing here is so important. But, you know who *really* needs to be here is . . ." followed by the list of their absent leaders. Just as frequently, I have watched as a top leader slips out of the room, thinking that if they stayed for the first few minutes, they have shown how much they support leadership development and have done their job. Unfortunately, they are sending the message that such development, continuous learning, and growth are for the rest of you, not for them. Their actions imply that once you reach the C-suite, you don't need to continue learning, or at least not shoulder to shoulder with your colleagues and direct reports.

On the positive flip side, I have seen the impact of leaders who choose to stay in the room, keeping their phones off and out of sight, taking notes, and participating in small group discussions and even playful improv exercises to improve their ability to embody agile leadership. These leaders demonstrate how much they value leadership development while also showing that they are still learning and growing themselves. Leaders who stay in the room and do the work are noticed and have an impact well beyond the few hours of shared experience.

Leaders who stay in the room and do the work are noticed and have an impact well beyond the few hours of shared experience.

Leading and Learning with Agility for a Dynamic Future

Because you are still reading, I assume you are a leader who chooses to stay in the room. You understand that now, more than ever, you need EALs at all levels of your organization to sustain your ability to stay in the game, and you take the lead by modeling the mindset and behaviors you want to see. You also know that while others in your organization may express frustrations about the barriers they encounter, you can help remove these barriers and champion a culture of Embodied Agile Leadership across your organization.

Most leaders do not lack positive intention, although many lack a clear picture of possibilities, pathways forward, and inspiration for their role. I've yet to encounter a leader who doesn't want her team members to perform at the top of their talent and have a fulfilling and what some call "frictionless" work experience. In these final pages, I introduce you to one last EAL and share a few possible starting points to help you bring Embodied Agile Leadership to life in your organization.

"Do I Know You?"

... I heard shouted from somewhere above me. I had just slid to a stop at the side of the run near the public NASTAR racecourse at Copper Mountain. I looked up in the direction of the question to see a friendly skier leaning over his poles.

"I don't know," I said, "Who are you?" a fair question, given that we could have been anybody underneath our helmets, goggles, and face masks. Paul Seitz introduced himself and, within a few minutes, we learned that our passion for ski racing was mutual. "You should come train with us over at Loveland!" Paul invited, "We have a great group over there, and you would fit right in. We race with the Rocky Mountain Masters all over the front range. You'd love it!"

My curiosity was piqued. The timing couldn't have been better, as I had plateaued in my development. I was ready for a new challenge, and I was searching for a Community out West that felt like a good fit. The end of the season was nearing, and I was leaving the area in a matter of days, but I promised to follow up soon and take Paul up on his invitation. This was not an idle commitment; Paul's affable enthusiasm had grabbed my attention and matched my desire to continue learning and improving.

When I returned home to Chicago, finding him didn't take long. In addition to being an avid masters racer, Paul was the vice president of the Rocky Mountain Masters and well connected to many people I knew (many of whom you have met in these pages). Over the summer, we exchanged text messages and talked by phone, and Paul shared more information and encouragement to help me get into the game. With each exchange, he committed to following up again, which he always did—not in a way that added pressure but that simply reflected my interest and enthusiasm.

It wasn't long before the snow flew again, and I was back in the mountains for more skiing, training, and racing. Within days of settling in, Paul texted to confirm the week's training schedule and offered to pick me up for the first session. On that maiden ride to training, I discovered that in addition to his lifelong passion for ski racing, Paul had spent 40 years at IBM in a variety of roles that tapped his in-depth education and unique skills, knowledge, and talent in engineering, mainframe computing, and customer engagement to lead complex international projects. Paul was a people person who had the leadership and technical skills to communicate equally effectively with his team members and his clients. Much of his success was because he had an embodied mindset, awareness, and understanding of human dynamics and emotional intelligence (which I discovered was the topic of his master's thesis)—and it showed.

Embodying Culture First and Last

Through each of the stories of EALs in action, you have seen how mindset is ingrained in the dynamics that enable leaders to stay in the game. Mindset is the wellspring of engagement and effective action and runs through all the examples of Embodied Agile Leadership. One way to think of culture is as the organizational mindset. Because, like mindset, it precedes and is necessary for sustained engagement. A culture of Embodied Agile Leadership is also the foundation for leading and learning with agility for a dynamic future.

Culture is the heartbeat of organizational life. This is because organizations are systems of human interaction. Yes, people organize for specific purposes and create structures, systems, and processes to achieve those purposes. However, these structural and operational elements are designed to enable the relational human system to be effective, and they reflect its culture.

One of my favorite descriptions of organizational culture is from Deal and Kennedy, who simply refer to it as "the way we do things around here."[1] Underpinning the way you do things is the repeated patterns of beliefs, attitudes, and values that your employees and colleagues witness and enact. The good news is that culture is socially constructed. Each day, you and all members of your organization have the choice to repeat or shift the attitudes and behaviors that construct your culture. As a visible leader in your organization, you have an outsized opportunity to impact the culture. This also means that when your actions are misaligned with the values you espouse, they are amplified, such as in my earlier example of leaders who step out of the room during an important leadership development program that they required their team to attend.

> **Each day, you and all members of your organization have the choice to repeat or shift the attitudes and behaviors that construct your culture.**

Setting Your Team Members Up for Success

If you think about your first time coming into a new organization or team, starting a new job, or testing the waters of a new endeavor, you likely remember some accompanying anxiety. The bigger the stretch or further out of your comfort zone, the greater the potential unknowns and pitfalls that could come with it. This was how I felt as I waited for Paul to pick me up in his mountain-weathered, green Ford Explorer that first day of training. I wondered if I would be welcomed and taken seriously or if I was completely delusional and getting in over my head.

Having an ambassador, such as Paul, who met me at the door, ushered me in, introduced me around, and helped me understand "how we do things around here," made the difference between these anxieties quickly dissipating or paralyzing me. Senior leaders and their team members who practice Embodied Agile Leadership understand that no matter how much experience and expertise a new member brings to their organization, they will also bring some degree of social and logistical trepidation. These anxieties can be compounded if the new member happens to be "the only" of their demographic in the group. EALs are cultural ambassadors who don't just focus on improving their own performance; they help create the conditions for others to succeed.

> **EALs are cultural ambassadors who don't just focus on improving their own performance; they help create the conditions for others to succeed.**

When we arrived at our training venue that first day, Paul walked me to the clubhouse, made a round of introductions, and let me know when and where I should be ready to load the lift. These might seem like small gestures, but on the first day of any new endeavor, the basic logistics of when, where, and how can loom large. Once our training group gathered at the top of the run that first day, everyone moved into action, helping set the course. Seeing that I wasn't sure how to contribute, Paul yelled out, "Pamela, shadow me!"

I skied down to where Paul was wrangling his share of gates to set when he promptly handed me a pair to insert into the holes the coach had drilled into the snow. As I followed his guidance, he leaned in and said, "I want you to do this, not just so you learn how the day goes, but so everyone else sees you helping. I want them to see that you are one of us." Paul knew that if I was to feel included in this close-knit group of longtime members, I needed not just to show up but to become a contributing member from day one. He wasn't doing this just for me. Paul's 40 years in business taught him that groups can continue to thrive only if all members contribute to its success.

Urgent and Necessary

Creating a culture and aligned systems and processes that support leading and learning with agility is urgent and necessary. In 2022, Gallup found that globally only 21% of employees are engaged at work, and only 33% report thriving in their overall well-being. These numbers are even worse in some regions, especially those hit hard by COVID-19, such as Southeast Asia, where only 11% report thriving.[2]

However, the impact of COVID-19 and the rapid shift to remote work account for just a small part of these numbers. You might be surprised that they are only slightly lower than before the pandemic. In another attention-getting study, Gallup found that people join companies but leave managers, attributing up to 70% of the variance in team productivity to the immediate manager.[3] While this data is alarming, it is actionable.

There is good reason to act—and to act now. In the 2022 study, Gallup also reported that "Business units with engaged workers have 23% higher profit than those with miserable workers. Additionally, teams with thriving workers see significantly lower absenteeism, turnover, and accidents and higher customer loyalty.

> The real fix is this simple: better leaders in the workplace. Managers need to be better listeners, coaches, and collabora-

tors. Great managers help colleagues learn and grow, recognize their colleagues for doing great work, and make them truly feel cared about. In environments like this, workers thrive.[4]

As a leader who shares responsibility for your organization's vision, mission, values, culture, and strategic priorities, you can do more than communicate the urgency and necessity of fostering a culture and best practices of Embodied Agile Leadership. You can translate this urgency into action.

Assess, Engage, and Act

With the urgent case above as motivation and Paul as inspiration, let's understand how you, as an influential leader, can help foster a culture and climate in which EALs at all levels of your organization can thrive. I recommend using the *Embodied Reflection and Action Framework* that you've become familiar with to assess your current organizational reality, engage your employees and colleagues (referred to as "your team," going forward) to discuss your insights, and prioritize action.

ASSESS What is Going On

Depending on the size and scope of your organization or team, you may choose to conduct a formal or informal assessment. Whether you gather information by informally "walking around," checking in with your team members via one-on-one meetings, or conducting a formal assessment, the goal is the same: to discover the current state of Embodied Agile Leadership in your organization and if the way you are doing things fosters a culture in which your EALs can thrive.

Ask What? and Gut?

These stages of your inquiry will help you understand *what* is going on and *how your team is feeling* about what is going on. Focus your inquiry on how each of the dynamics of Embodied Agile Leadership is reflected in your culture at the team or organizational level. Below, I translate the individual embodied leadership dynamics to the organizational level and share some sample questions to help get your inquiry underway.

- **Meaningful Identify = Purpose.** Find out if your team members feel valued for their Meaningful Identity and what they care about. Is their individual purpose and value aligned with your mission and the value they generate for your stakeholders?

- **Community = People.** Find out if new team members experience being welcomed into your organization's Community. Are they set up for success in a way that both helps them understand "the way you do things around here" while also welcoming their questions and fresh ideas? Do they experience belonging? Do they know they would be missed if they were not there? Have you created opportunities and spaces for meaningful interaction where people can make connections and generate positive relational energy?

- **Competition = Continuous Learning and Improvement.** Find out if you foster a culture of learning and improvement across the organization. Do your team members participate in various learning activities that directly improve their competence, capacity, and confidence to work at the top of their talent and lead with agility? Are they intrinsically motivated to learn and grow? Is this growth and the value it generates recognized and rewarded in a way that team members find meaningful and motivating?

- **Commitment = Prioritizing Employee and Stakeholder Value.** Find out if you are continually assessing and adapting in response to the changing needs of your team members and stakeholders. Do you engage them to listen to and discuss their experiences, insights, and ideas? Do you reprioritize your strategy and tactics based on those insights to improve team member and customer experience and stakeholder value?

ENGAGE Your Colleagues in a "So What?" Conversation

Years of work on organizational change initiatives have shown me that it is human nature for people to push back on changes they did not have an opportunity to co-create. Resist the temptation to generate a report or slide deck summarizing the findings of your assessment and then file it away or share it only with your senior leadership colleagues. Instead, engage your team members in a conversation to discover the strengths and opportunities within the data you have collected. These conversations can happen at the team level and be scaled in meaningful ways across the organization. Skip this process at your peril.

ACT Based on Your "Now What?" Decisions

High engagement leads to a clear WIIFM and increased co-ownership of both the process and outcomes of new initiatives. Tap the energy and momentum of your engaged conversations to propel effective action. Now is not the time to summarize team member suggestions and send them back to the C-suite. Instead, as you explore your strengths and opportunities, focus on the most engaged participants; these are your current and emerging EALs. Encourage them to take the lead and help gather support for proposed changes. Demonstrate that you have their back as they negotiate the organizational system and inevitable obstacles. Connect these EALs to other leaders and influencers in your Relational Web who share their values and Commitment and can help get things done. Celebrate the engagement, as well as small and large wins along the way, and shine a light on all who step up to co-create an Embodied Agile Leadership culture and practices across your organization.

Recruit, Recognize, Reinforce, and Retain Embodied Agile Leaders

If you are familiar with the core concepts of *The Agility Shift,* you know how important it is for you, as a C-suite leader or influencer, to Recruit, Recognize, Reinforce, and Retain your top talent.[5] In an agile organization, these responsibilities cannot be left only to your HR department; they must be shared by leaders across functions. Even if you are already involved in these efforts, read on as I review these imperatives with an expanded focus on Embodied Agile Leadership.

Recruit and Welcome

The first secret of recruiting is to know where to find your potential EALs. I had flattered myself that Paul had called out to me on the mountainside that day because he noticed my awesome turns. I later learned that he regularly scoped out the racecourse to recruit new members for the Rocky Mountain Masters. Paul knew that he was most likely to find prospective racers near the racecourse, where he could also see them in action, engage them in conversation, and gauge their interest and enthusiasm. EALs in business also seek out highly engaged leaders where they are most likely to be connecting, learning, and innovating. Identify the gathering spots, practice venues, idea-sharing forums, and training grounds in your business; then stake out a spot and holler across your mountain to get the attention of worthy prospects.

Of course, recruiting is much more than identifying potential EALs. It is also the time to assess if your opportunity is well aligned with your candidate's Meaningful Identity and if your team and organization is a place where they can continue learning and growing, and deepen their purpose, passion, pleasure, and play.

When you are confident that the answer is a resounding "Yes!" the best part begins. Assure that your new team member is welcomed with your best version of radical hospitality, introduced in Chapter 5. Beyond individual introductions, this may include public welcomes that amplify why you are so excited about what your new EAL is bringing to the team. These efforts must go beyond your formal onboarding process; they must be relational, not simply transactional. After my first few training sessions, Paul pulled me aside to tell me that "we are so glad you are here," and again welcomed me more publicly during the awards party after my first race. Don't assume that people will know they are welcome: say it, show it, and show it again.

Don't assume that people will know they are welcome: say it, show it, and show it again.

Paul's recruiting persistence and robust welcome made all the difference as I listened in on my first pre-race orientation meeting. I felt a wave of nausea as the race director ran through his checklist of reminders, including an assurance that there would be ample "Stop Bleed Kits" on the course and that a ski patrol team with toboggan would be at the top of the course to respond in seconds "if there are any issues" during the race. Neither of these items were part of the routine for our tamer Midwest races. I'll admit a brief impulse to slip out the side door at that point but was able to embrace my anxious confidence and have a winning first race, cheered on by Paul and other club members. It is no coincidence that the Rocky Mountain Masters has had the highest number of new members across the United States in recent years. People want to be part of positive endeavors where they feel welcomed and valued.

Recognize and Reinforce

These two imperatives go hand in hand because recognition helps reinforce Embodied Agile Leadership success. Those who co-create your success come to life when you shine a light on their animating values, mindset, and behaviors. Stories of Embodied Agile Leadership get our attention and inspire us to live into our Meaningful Identity in new and impactful ways. As a senior leader, you can call significant attention to the EALs whose initiative demonstrates your values and contributes to positive outcomes within your organization and for your external stakeholders. Who stood at the bottom of the course, cheering me on that first race day? Paul, of course, who also spurred more shouts of encouragement from fellow racers. Later that day, as I stretched my aching muscles, my phone buzzed with more encouraging texts. While I will be the first to tell you of all the things I still need to work on, the unbridled joyful encouragement made all the difference in my feeling like I deserved to be there and had found a Community that shared my Commitment and where I would be stretched to continue learning and improving through rigorous Competition. You don't need to wait for just the right moment or formal public opportunity to recognize Embodied Agile Leadership success. Recognize, encourage, and amplify early and often.

As a senior leader, you can call significant attention to the EALs whose initiative demonstrates your values and contributes to positive outcomes within your organization and for your external stakeholders.

Reinforcement Through Learning and Improvement. As a senior leader, you have a keen interest in ensuring your team members stay competitive. EALs are intrinsically motivated to continue learning and improving. By championing a range of new learning and growth opportunities to support their continued success, you are reinforcing the values and best practices of Embodied Agile Leadership. I often invoke the fitness metaphor when it comes to developing EALs. Just like we cannot sign up for a ten-week fitness program and, on completion, expect continued results if we return to our old habits, leaders cannot sustain Embodied Agile Leadership without a consistent variety of "workouts."

When resources allow, it can be incredibly valuable to tap seasoned expertise to help guide your team. However, there is no need to delay. There are many ways to reinforce continuous learning and leadership development by working with your available resources. A few examples include inviting your team members to share their discoveries via informal gatherings, onsite or virtual lunch 'n learns, and other shared platforms. Use existing platforms to share short articles and videos that are getting your attention and that reinforce key dimensions of Embodied Agile Leadership. Invite EALs to share their agile leadership success stories and lessons learned in a short blog or vlog post. Create peer coaching opportunities and what is sometimes called "reverse mentoring" to foster knowledge sharing and help your team members expand and diversify their Relational Web. One of the most powerful ways to reinforce continuous learning is to encourage team members to take on stretch assignments to improve their skills, knowledge, and learning agility. These are just a few of countless ways you can recognize and reinforce Embodied Agile Leadership and ensure your team members are fit to respond effectively to unexpected and unplanned challenges and opportunities.

Retain and Reengage

EALs want to stay where they are valued and have opportunities to continue to learn and grow that are aligned with their Meaningful Identity and contribute to a purpose that is bigger than themselves. While it's true that great talent joins organizations and leaves managers, great talent also *stays* with managers whom they trust and who support their continued growth. For this reason, retaining EALs *almost* takes care of itself if you are intentional in Recruiting and Welcoming, Recognizing, and Reinforcing the success of your team members. I say that retention *almost* takes care of itself because we know that the present and future are dynamic. Even your most engaged team members have a range of opportunities, and savvy recruiters, like Paul, know where to find *your* talent and how to tempt them to make a change.

EALs create that all-important relational energy and discover how things are really going so they can help improve their team members' work experience and effectiveness. For this reason, in addition to co-creating a culture of Embodied Agile Leadership, recruiting and welcoming, recognizing and reinforcing your talent, you need to regularly engage and reengage your team members in direct conversation. HR professionals sometimes call these conversations "stay interviews." Unlike exit interviews that gather insight into employee experiences when they are walking out the door, stay interviews are intended to do just that: ensure that your talented team members stay with you because they feel part of a dynamic Community, have rich opportunities for Competition via learning and improvement, and can prioritize the Commitment needed to play the game at the top of their talent.

Start Where You Are

Whether you currently occupy the C-suite or inhabit any other seat in your organization, you have the power to foster Embodied Agile Leadership through your attitudes, behaviors, and actions. Start where you are today with compassion and generosity for yourself and others. You may start by slowing down to reflect on your Meaningful Identity and the times in your life when you are most engaged and energized in your game. You may start by reengaging with a Community where you have enjoyed playing or seek out a new one where people gather for shared purpose, passion, play, and pleasure. You may start by exploring new opportunities for Competition with yourself or others through learning and growth. Or you may start by renewing your Commitment to prioritizing ways of being and doing that generate the most value and happiness for you and your stakeholders. It does not matter which step you take. It only matters that you take it.

ACKNOWLEDGMENTS

As you likely guessed, writing *Staying in the Game* was more than an intellectual endeavor for me; it was an opportunity to engage more deeply in the four Ps of the game (play, purpose, passion, and pleasure) and discover how they play out on the alpine racecourse and many other high-stakes frontiers. Along the way, I encountered and formed connections with kindred spirits on the mountains and across industries. I could not have stayed in this game without abundant support and encouragement over the years I spent inquiring, incubating, and refining the themes that ultimately shaped this book.

This support is led by my unflagging first and last reader and head cheerleader, my wife, Carol Semrad. Many others served as sounding boards during concept development and at various stages in the process, starting with my friend, colleague, and thinking partner, Catherine Marienau, Ph.D., who never wavered in her encouragement and insight over cherished dinners and zoom calls. Along the way, several others chimed in sharing their guidance, experience, and wisdom, including Ann Farlee, Laurie Harper, Dan Hibbler, Ph.D., Perry Pidgeon Hooks, Jill Pollack, and Michelle Sanford. As the manuscript evolved, I also was lucky to have the keen and thoughtful editorial eye and encouraging ear of Susan Aiello, DVM, ELS to guide me through every twist and turn, and the collaborative spirit and book design talents of George Stevens at G Sharp Design, LLC.

Beyond the embodied agile leaders highlighted in the book, I am grateful for the incredible communities of athletes and coaches I have been lucky enough to train and play with, including the Chicago Metropolitan Ski Council Racing and WoW! (Women of Wilmot), NASTAR, Rocky Mountain Masters, Ron Emery, and the Loveland Ski Club, Dave Greggory, Matt Fox, and Peak Performance Ski Camp, Justine Gianandrea, Allison Andrews, Jenn Lyons, and the Saturday morning yoga group, as well as inspiring people who supported this journey in more ways than they may know, including Johnse Holt, Sheena Lawrick, Rene Lederman, Allison Morgan, Amy Nelson, Michael Pontarelli, Heather Riordan, Judith Schneebeck, Pat Staszak, and Mari Pat Varga.

Thank you, too, to Jasmine Claycomb for your radical hospitality and additional insights, as well as to Will Bernau, Denise Sedivy, Tracy Stevenson, and Vincene Verdun, who also made the time to share their experiences with athletics, masters racing, and leadership providing valuable background.

I am deeply grateful to all the other embodied agile leaders on the mountain and across the business landscape who generously shared their stories and wisdom with me. I continue to learn from your inspiring example and commitment to staying in the game.

ABOUT THE AUTHOR

Pamela Meyer, Ph.D., is a catalyst for agile leadership and innovation. With a deep-rooted passion for collaboration first cultivated through leading creative teams in the arts, she now helps leaders and teams be effective in high-stakes, dynamic business environments. With more than 20 years of experience improving results informed by extensive research, she equips Fortune 500 to Fortune 50 companies and beyond with high-impact approaches. Her transformative guidance helps leaders and teams to make a mindset and practice shift for tangible outcomes, while cultivating thriving workplaces where leaders at all levels perform at the top of their talent.

Pamela is a sought-after keynote speaker and thought leader who inspires audiences worldwide with engaging learning experiences and actionable ideas for sustainable results. Her most popular keynote and custom program themes include:

- Making the Agility Shift
- Leading and Learning with Agility for a Dynamic Future
- Leading (and Following) Agile Teams

Staying in the Game is Pamela's fifth book on innovation, learning, and change. Her other books include *The Agility Shift*, *From Workplace* to *Playspace*, and *Quantum Creativity*, and she has published many articles, book chapters, and blog posts.

In addition to her work as a consultant, author, and speaker, Pamela spent many years teaching at DePaul University, where she also served as the founding director of the Center to Advance Education for Adults, and a Faculty Fellow at the Center for Creativity and Innovation, part of the Driehaus College of Business and the Kellstadt Graduate School of Business.

A lifelong learner, Pamela holds a doctorate and master's degree in Human and Organizational Systems, a master's in creativity and innovation, and a BFA in theater production. She also practices staying in the game as a masters alpine ski racer, cyclist, aspiring swimmer, and through other fitness and stretch learning experiences, including travel adventures with her wife.

Connect and Learn More

Visit: Pamela-meyer.com

Contact Pamela Meyer to invite her to speak at your next event or work with your leaders:
https://pamela-meyer.com/pamela-meyer-contact/

Read Pamela's Blog:
https://pamela-meyer.com/the-agile-blog/

Follow Pamela:
  LinkedIn: https://www.linkedin.com/in/pamelameyerphd
  Facebook: https://www.facebook.com/pamelameyerphd/
  X/Twitter & Instagram: @pamelameyerphd

A portion of "Staying in the Game" proceeds are donated to expand access and diversify participation in youth snow sports and arts-based education programs.

CHAPTER NOTES

All URLs listed were current and live on date accessed or book publication date.

Introduction

1. Developed by SKI Magazine in 1968, NASTAR (NAtional STAndard Race) is the largest recreational ski and snowboard race program globally. Since the program's inception, more than 6 million skier and snowboarder racer days have been recorded. This is accomplished by establishing a National Standard for all races based on the standard set by professional racers at the start of each season, https://www.nastar.com/about.

2. J. Evelyn Orr, "Forget the Score. Just Play" 2017, https://www.kornferry.com/institute/forget-the-score-just-play.

3. "Work Trend Index: Microsoft's Latest Research on the Ways We Work," accessed July 14, 2022, https://www.microsoft.com/en-us/worklab/work-trend-index.

4. "The Great Attrition Is Making Hiring Harder. Are You Searching the Right Talent Pools?" McKinsey & Company, July 13, 2022, https://www.mckinsey.com/business-functions/people-and-organizational-performance/our-insights/the-great-attrition-is-making-hiring-harder-are-you-searching-the-right-talent-pools?fs=e&s=cl.

Chapter 1

1. Karl Weick, "The Aesthetic of Imperfection in Orchestras and Organizations," in *Organizational Improvisation*, eds. Miguel Pina e Cunha,

Joao Vieira da Cunha, and Ken N. Kamoche (New York: Routledge, 2002), 166.

2. Pamela Meyer, *From Workplace to Playspace: Innovating, Learning and Changing Through Dynamic Engagement* (New York: John Wiley & Sons, 2010).

3. Beth A. Bechky and Gerardo A. Okhuysen, "Expecting the Unexpected? How SWAT Officers and Film Crews Handle Surprises," *Academy of Management Journal* 54, no. 2 (April 1, 2011): 239-61. https://doi.org/10.5465/amj.2011.60263060.

4. Karl E. Weick, "The Collapse of Sensemaking in Organizations: The Mann Gulch Disaster," *Administrative Science Quarterly* 38, no. 4 (December 1, 1993): 628. https://doi.org/10.2307/2393339.

Chapter 2

1. If you are still in the process of identifying your game (Play, Purpose, Passion, and Pleasure), revisit the coaching suggestions at the end of Chapter 1.

2. Roy Maurer, "Turnover 'Tsunami' Expected Once Pandemic Ends," SHRM, March 12, 2021, https://www.shrm.org/resourcesandtools/hr-topics/talent-acquisition/pages/turnover-tsunami-expected-once-pandemic-ends.aspx.

3. Dan Seligson, JewishBoston, "Peace Through Backgammon: Ask Me Anything With Zaki Djemal," June 8, 2017, http://www.jewishboston.com/read/peace-through-backgammon-ask-me-anything-with-zaki-djemal/.

4. Seligson, "Peace Through Backgammon," 2017.

5. "All of Us," http://kulna.org/en/homepage.

6. Grant Soosalu, Suzanne Henwood, and Arun Deo, "Head, Heart, and Gut in Decision Making: Development of a Multiple Brain Preference Questionnaire," SAGE Open 9, no. 1 (January 2019), https://doi.org/10.1177/2158244019837439.

7. Carl Sagan, Neil Degrasse Tyson, and Ann Druyan, *Cosmos* (New York: Ballantine Books, 2013).

8. Pamela Meyer, *The Agility Shift: Creating Agile and Effective Leaders, Teams and Organizations* (New York: Routledge, 2016).

9. "Five Whys and Five Hows," American Society for Quality, https://asq.org/quality-resources/five-whys.

Chapter 3

1. Cindy Dietrich, "Decision Making: Factors That Influence Decision Making, Heuristics Used, and Decision Outcomes." *Inquiries Journal* 2, no. 02, (January 1, 2010), http://www.inquiriesjournal.com/a?id=180.

2. David Rock, "SCARF: A Brain-Based Model for Collaborating with and Influencing Others." *Neuroleadership Journal* 1, no. 1, (2008): 78-87.

3. "Odds of Dying - Injury Facts." 2023. *Injury Facts*. (March 1, 2023), https://injuryfacts.nsc.org/all-injuries/preventable-death-overview/odds-of-dying/?

4. "Odds of Dying - Injury Facts," 2023.

5. Arnrisha Vaish, Tobias Grossmann, and Amanda L. Woodward, "Not All Emotions Are Created Equal: The Negativity Bias in Social-Emotional Development." *Psychological Bulletin* 134, no. 3 (May 1, 2008): 383–403, https://doi.org/10.1037/0033-2909.134.3.383.

6. Erin McDowell and Avery Hartmans, "The Rise and Fall of Sears. Once the World's Largest Retailer, It Now Has Just 15 Stores Left. Here's How Changing Consumer Habits Took down a One-Time Powerhouse." *Business Insider*, (December 19, 2022), https://www.businessinsider.com/rise-and-fall-of-sears-bankruptcy-store-closings.

7. Koon K. Teo, Scott A. Lear, Shofiqul Islam, Prem Mony, Mahshid Dehghan, Wei Li, Annika Rosengren, et al, "Prevalence of a Healthy Lifestyle Among Individuals With Cardiovascular Disease in High-, Middle- and Low-Income Countries." *JAMA* 309, no. 15 (April 17, 2013): 1613, https://doi.org/10.1001/jama.2013.3519.

8. "Tobacco: Health Benefits of Smoking Cessation," (May 24, 2022), https://www.who.int/tobacco/quitting/benefits/en/.

9. Antoine Bechara, "The Role of Emotion in Decision-Making: Evidence from Neurological Patients with Orbitofrontal Damage." *Brain and Cognition* 55, no. 1 (June 1, 2004): 30–40, https://doi.org/10.1016/j.bandc.2003.04.001.

10. Nasir H. Naqvi, Baba Shiv, and Antoine Bechara, "The Role of Emotion in Decision Making." *Current Directions in Psycho-*

logical Science 15, no. 5 (October 1, 2006): 260–64, https://doi.org/10.1111/j.1467-8721.2006.00448.x.

11. Andrew J. Elliot, and Kennon M. Sheldon, "Avoidance Achievement Motivation: A Personal Goals Analysis." *Journal of Personality and Social Psychology* 73, no. 1 (January 1, 1997): 171–85, https://doi.org/10.1037/0022-3514.73.1.171.

Chapter 4

1. Developed by SKI Magazine in 1968, NASTAR (NAtional STAndard Race) is the largest recreational ski and snowboard race program globally. Since the program's inception, more than 6 million skier and snowboarder racer days have been recorded. This is accomplished by establishing a National Standard for all races based on the standard set by professional racers at the start of each season, https://www.nastar.com/about.

2. Pamela Meyer, *The Agility Shift: Creating Agile and Effective Leaders, Teams and Organizations*, (Routledge, 2016), 9-10.

3. FrieslandCampina Ingredients is one of the world's leading manufacturers of high-quality, value-added, functional nutritional ingredients and solutions.

4. Joseph E. LeDoux, *Synaptic Self: How Our Brains Become Who We Are.* (New York: Viking Adult, 2002).

5. Allison S. Troy, Frank H. Wilhelm, Amanda J. Shallcross, and Iris B. Mauss, "Seeing the Silver Lining: Cognitive Reappraisal Ability Moderates the Relationship between Stress and Depressive Symptoms." *Emotion* 10, no. 6 (December 1, 2010), 783–95. https://doi.org/10.1037/a0020262.

6. Alan D. Meyer, Peter J. Frost, Karl E. Weick, and Philip H. Mirvis, "Variations on a Theme—Practice Improvisation." *Organization Science* 9, no. 5 (May 1, 1998), 586–92. https://doi.org/10.1287/orsc.9.5.586.

7. Anna Johnson, "Gut Feelings: The World of the Second Brain," *The Lancet Gastroenterology & Hepatology* 3, no. 8 (August 2018): 536, https://doi.org/10.1016/s2468-1253(18)30209-7.

8. To understand the difference between overall business agility and specific Agile Frameworks (sometimes referred to as "Agile with a capital A"), see, Pamela Meyer, "Agile 101: Agility vs. Agile" [Blog post], https://pamela-meyer.com/agile-101-part-1-of-3-agile-vs-agility/

Chapter 5

1. J. Patrick Williams and Kaylan C. Schwarz, *Studies on the Social Construction of Identity and Authenticity*. (Milton Park, Abingdon, Oxon; New York, NY: Routledge, 2020).

2. Robert Kegan, "Making Meaning: The Constructive-Developmental Approach to Persons and Practice." *The Personnel and Guidance Journal* 58, no. 5 (January 1, 1980): 373–80, https://doi.org/10.1002/j.2164-4918.1980.tb00416.x.

3. Chris Dixon, "Dorian Paskowitz Dies at 93: Doctor and Surfer Lived an Endless Summer." *The New York Times* (November 15, 2014). https://www.nytimes.com/2014/11/15/sports/dorian-paskowitz-doctor-and-surfer-who-lived-an-endless-summer-dies-at-93.html?_r=0.

4. Gad Yair, "What Keeps Them Running? The 'Circle of Commitment' of Long Distance Runners." *Leisure Studies* 11, no. 3 (September 1, 1992): 257–70, https://doi.org/10.1080/02614369200390131.

5. Pamela Meyer, *From Workplace to Playspace: Innovating, Learning and Changing Through Dynamic Engagement*. (New York: John Wiley & Sons, 2010).

6. Pamela Meyer, "Embodied Learning at Work: Making the Mindset Shift from Workplace to Playspace," in *Bodies of Knowledge: Embodied Learning in Adult Education: New Directions for Adult and Continuing Education*, ed., Lawrence, Randee Lipson. *Number 134*. (New York: John Wiley & Sons, 2012), 25-32.

7. "Baby Boomers Born from 1957 to 1964 Held an Average of 12.4 Jobs from Ages 18 to 54 : The Economics Daily: U.S. Bureau of Labor Statistics," September 3, 2021, https://www.bls.gov/opub/ted/2021/baby-boomers-born-from-1957-to-1964-held-an-average-of-12-4-jobs-from-ages-18-to-54.htm.

8. For more information and to access the 100s of podcasts visit: https://womenover70.com/

9. Alison Wade, "T-Mobile CEO Offers Unexpected Performance Bonuses at NYC Half." *Runner's World*, March 3, 2022, https://www.runnersworld.com/races-places/a20852069/t-mobile-ceo-offers-unexpected-performance-bonuses-at-nyc-half/.

10. Aaron Pressman, "Inside T-Mobile's Big, Brash Comeback." *Fortune*, June 8, 2021, https://fortune.com/2018/02/15/best-companies-t-mobile.

11. Chris Schleier, "How T-Mobile's John Legere Ripped Up Your Wireless Contract." *Investor's Business Daily*, September 16, 2021. https://www.investors.com/news/management/leaders-and-success/john-legere-of-t-mobile-ripped-up-your-wireless-contract/.

12. Schleier, "How T-Mobile's John Legere," 2021.

13. Pamela Meyer, *The Agility Shift: Creating Agile and Effective Leaders, Teams, and Organizations*. (New York: Routledge, 2016).

14. Mursion, "WEBINAR: The Agility Shift: T-Mobile Develops Leaders for a VUCA World (w/ Melissa Lanier)," January 7, 2020, https://www.youtube.com/watch?v=Vk99y29jC5w.

15. Aaron Pressman, "John Legere Will Go down in Corporate History as One of the Greatest Turnaround Stories of All Time." *Fortune*, February 12, 2020, https://fortune.com/2020/02/12/john-legere-will-go-down-in-corporate-history-as-one-of-the-greatest-turnaround-stories-of-all-time/.

16. Habitat for Humanity, "Our Mission, Vision and Principles | Habitat for Humanity," n.d. https://www.habitat.org/about/mission-and-vision.

17. The Adaway Group, "About Us: The Adaway Group - Building Inclusive Workplaces," February 15, 2022, https://adawaygroup.com/about/.

Chapter 6

1. "Explore Careers in Fashion at H&M | H&M Careers United States." H&M Careers United States, Accessed August 13, 2022, https://career.hm.com/us-en.

2. "Glassdoor's Diversity and Inclusion Workplace Survey." Glassdoor Blog, last modified September 29, 2020, https://www.glassdoor.com/blog/glassdoors-diversity-and-inclusion-workplace-survey/.

3. ToossiMitra, "Labor Force Projections to 2024: The Labor Force Is Growing, but Slowly: Monthly Labor Review: U.S. Bureau of Labor Statistics," December 8, 2015, https://www.bls.gov/opub/mlr/2015/article/labor-force-projections-to-2024.htm.

4. Scott Butterworth, "Anna Deavere Smith to Deliver Scott and Fender Lecture," June 1, 2021, https://resources.depaul.edu/newsline/sections/debuzz/Pages/deavere-smith.aspx.

5. Robert B. Slocum and Victoria Slocum, "Radical Hospitality and Faith Inclusion: Lessons from St. Benedict." *Journal of Disability and Religion*, (April 3, 2021): 181-190, https://doi.org/10.1080/23312521.2020.1716917.

6. United States Census Bureau QuickFacts, "U.S. Census Bureau QuickFacts: United States." Census Bureau QuickFacts. Accessed November 18, 2022,

7. https://www.census.gov/quickfacts/fact/table/US/PST045221.

8. National Ski Areas Association, "U.S. Downhill Sports Participant Demographics 2021/22," October 2022, https://nsaa.org/webdocs/Media_Public/IndustryStats/Skier_Demographics_2022.pdf

9. "Home - National Brotherhood of Skiers, Inc.," https://www.nbs.org/about/.

10. Emile Durkheim, *Suicide, a Study in Sociology*. (Minneapolis: Franklin Classics Trade Press, 2018).

11. Elizabeth Blackburn and Elissa Epel, *The Telomere Effect: A Revolutionary Approach to Living Younger, Healthier, Longer*. (London: Orion, 2018).

12. "Suicide Data and Statistics | Suicide | CDC," June 28, 2022, https://www.cdc.gov/suicide/suicide-data-statistics.html.

13. Clay Routledge, "Opinion | Suicides Have Increased. Is This an Existential Crisis?" *The New York Times*, June 23, 2018. https://www.nytimes.com/2018/06/23/opinion/sunday/suicide-rate-existential-crisis.html.

14. "SkiMeisters – Exceptionally Active Adults 55 & Older." https://theskimeisters.org/.

15. Geraldine Aubert and Peter M. Lansdorp, "Telomeres and Aging." *Physiological Reviews* 88, no. 2 (April 1, 2008): 557–79. https://doi.org/10.1152/physrev.00026.2007.

16. Karen D. Lincoln, Donald A. Lloyd, and Ann W. Nguyen, "Social Relationships and Salivary Telomere Length Among Middle-Aged and Older African American and White Adults." *The Journals of Gerontology: Series B* 74, no. 6 (August 21, 2019): 1053–61. https://doi.org/10.1093/geronb/gbx049.

17. Elizabeth Blackburn and Elissa Epel, *The Telomere Effect: A Revolutionary Approach to Living Younger, Healthier, Longer*. (London: Orion, 2018).

18. Alan D. Meyer, Peter J. Frost, Karl E. Weick, and Philip H. Mirvis, "Variations on a Theme—Practice Improvisation." *Organization Science* 9, no. 5 (May 1, 1998): 586–92, https://doi.org/10.1287/orsc.9.5.586.

19. Ryan P. Adams, Jonathan Bruce Santo, and William M. Bukowski, "The Presence of a Best Friend Buffers the Effects of Negative Experiences." *Developmental Psychology* 47, no. 6 (September 5, 2011): 1786–91, https://doi.org/10.1037/a0025401.

20. Simone Schnall, Kent D. Harber, Jeanine K. Stefanucci, and Dennis R. Proffitt, "Social Support and the Perception of Geographical Slant." *Journal of Experimental Social Psychology* 44, no. 5 (September 1, 2008): 1246–55, https://doi.org/10.1016/j.jesp.2008.04.011.

21. Albert Bandura, "Social Learning Theory." *Contemporary Sociology* 7, no. 1 (January 1, 1977): 84, https://doi.org/10.2307/2065952.

22. Öznur Gülen Ertosun and Oya Erdil, "The Effects of Loneliness on Employees' Commitment and Intention to Leave." *Procedia - Social and Behavioral Sciences* 41 (January 1, 2012): 469–76, https://doi.org/10.1016/j.sbspro.2012.04.057.

23. Pamela Meyer, "Tap the Agile Power of Your Relational Web." July 20, 2018, https://pamela-meyer.com/tap-agile-power-relational-web.

24. Charles Duhigg, "What Google Learned From Its Quest to Build the Perfect Team." *The New York Times*, February 25, 2016, https://www.nytimes.com/2016/02/28/magazine/what-google-learned-from-its-quest-to-build-the-perfect-team.html?_r=0.

25. Matthew Dixon, "How T-Mobile Brought Collaboration to Customer Service." *Harvard Business Review*, October 23, 2018, https://hbr.org/2018/11/reinventing-customer-service.

26. Angela Moscaritolo, "T-Mobile Leads on Customer Satisfaction, Sprint Comes in Last." *PCMAG*, June 4, 2019, https://www.pcmag.com/news/t-mobile-leads-on-customer-satisfaction-sprint-comes-in-last.

27. Scott Moritz, "T-Mobile Customer Service Is Getting as Bad as All the Others." Bloomberg.Com, December 6, 2021, https://www.bloomberg.com/news/articles/2021-12-06/t-mobile-customer-service-is-getting-as-bad-as-all-the-others.

28. Harry T. Reis, Stephanie D. O'Keefe, and Richard D. Lane, "Fun Is More Fun When Others Are Involved." *The Journal of Positive Psychology* 12, no. 6 (November 2, 2017): 547–57, https://doi.org/10.1080/17439760.2016.1221123.

29. Katherine A. Karl, Joy V. Peluchette, and Leda McIntyre Hall, "Give Them Something to Smile About: A Marketing Strategy for Recruiting and Retaining Volunteers." *Journal of Nonprofit & Public Sector Marketing* 20, no. 1 (September 8, 2008): 71–96, https://doi.org/10.1080/10495140802165360.

30. Emma Seppälä, "The Best Leaders Have a Contagious Positive Energy." *Harvard Business Review*, April 4, 2023, https://hbr.org/2022/04/the-best-leaders-have-a-contagious-positive-energy.

31. Seppälä, "The Best Leaders," 2023, digital reprint, 3.

Chapter 7

1. Richard M. Ryan and Edward L. Deci, "Self-Determination Theory and the Facilitation of Intrinsic Motivation, Social Development, and Well-Being." *American Psychologist* 55, no. 1 (January 1, 2000): 68–78, https://doi.org/10.1037/0003-066x.55.1.68.

2. Teresa Amabile and Steven Kramer, *The Progress Principle: Using Small Wins to Ignite Joy, Engagement, and Creativity at Work*. (Cambridge, MA: Harvard Business Press, 2011).

3. Delia O'Hara, "The Intrinsic Motivation of Richard Ryan and Edward Deci." *American Psychological Association*, December 18, 2017, https://www.apa.org/members/content/intrinsic-motivation.

4. O'Hara, "The Intrinsic Motivation," December 18, 2017.

5. Eric Almquist, "The 30 Elements of Consumer Value: A Hierarchy." *Harvard Business Review.* November 10, 2021. https://hbr.org/2016/09/the-elements-of-value.

6. Christopher P. Niemiec, Richard M. Ryan, and Edward L. Deci, "The Path Taken: Consequences of Attaining Intrinsic and Extrinsic Aspirations in Post-College Life." *Journal of Research in Personality* 43, no. 3 (June 1, 2009): 291–306, https://doi.org/10.1016/j.jrp.2008.09.001.

7. Teresa Amabile and Steven Kramer, *The Progress Principle: Using Small Wins to Ignite Joy, Engagement, and Creativity at Work.* (Cambridge, MA: Harvard Business Press, 2011).

8. Alfie Kohn, *Punished by Rewards: The Trouble with Gold Stars, Incentive Plans, A's, Praise, and Other Bribes.* (Boston: Houghton Mifflin, 2018).

9. Carol Dweck, *Mindset - Updated Edition: Changing The Way You Think To Fulfil Your Potential.* (New York: Hachette, 2017).

10. Angela L. Duckworth, Christopher Peterson, Michael R. Matthews, and Dennis D. Kelly, 2007. "Grit: Perseverance and Passion for Long-Term Goals." *Journal of Personality and Social Psychology* 92 no. 6 (2007): 1087–1101. https://doi.org/10.1037/0022-3514.92.6.1087.

11. Robert W. Eichinger and Michael V. Lombardo, "Learning Agility as a Prime Indicator of Potential." *Human Resource Planning* 27, no. 4 (December 1, 2004): 12, https://www.questia.com/library/journal/1G1-126653494/learning-agility-as-a-prime-indicator-of-potential.

12. Nevitt Sanford, *Self and Society: Social Change and Individual Development.* (Piscataway, NJ: Transaction Publishers, 2017).

13. Teresa Amabile and Steven Kramer, *The Progress Principle: Using Small Wins to Ignite Joy, Engagement, and Creativity at Work.* (Cambridge, MA: Harvard Business Press, 2011).

14. Kathleen Taylor and Catherine Marienau, *Facilitating Learning with the Adult Brain in Mind: A Conceptual and Practical Guide*. (New York: John Wiley & Sons, 2016).

15. Kumar M. Mehta, "The Most Mentally Tough People Apply the 1% 'Marginal Gains' Rule, Says Performance Expert— Here's How It Works." *CNBC*, February 23, 2021, https://www.cnbc.com/2021/02/23/how-to-be-mentally-tough-use-the-1percent-marginal-gains-rule-says-performance-expert.html.

Chapter 8

1. Michael D. Christian, Adela S. Garza, and Jerel E. Slaughter, "Work Engagement: A Quantitative Review and Test of Its Relations with Task and Contextual Performance." *Personnel Psychology* 64, no. 1 (March 1, 2011): 89–136, https://doi.org/10.1111/j.1744-6570.2010.01203.x.

2. E.C. Soane, "Leadership and Employee Engagement," In *Employee Engagement in Theory and Practice*. Eds. Catherine Truss, Kerstin Alfes, Rick Delbridge, Amanda Shantz, and Emma Soane. (Milton Park, Abingdon, Oxon; New York, NY: Routledge, 2013), 149-162.

3. Gary M. Burlingame, Addie Fuhriman, and Julie Mosier, "The Differential Effectiveness of Group Psychotherapy: A Meta-Analytic Perspective." *Group Dynamics: Theory, Research, and Practice* 7, no. 1 (March 1, 2003): 3–12, https://doi.org/10.1037/1089-2699.7.1.3.

4. Richard M. Ryan and Edward L. Deci, "Self-Determination Theory and the Facilitation of Intrinsic Motivation, Social Development, and Well-Being." *American Psychologist* 55, no. 1 (January 1, 2000): 68–78, https://doi.org/10.1037/0003-066x.55.1.68.

5. Ken Hodge, Justine Allen, and Liz Smellie, "Motivation in Masters Sport: Achievement and Social Goals." *Psychology of Sport and Exercise* 9, no. 2 (March 1, 2008): 157–76, https://doi.org/10.1016/j.psychsport.2007.03.002.

6. Harry T. Reis, Stephanie D. O'Keefe, and Richard D. Lane, "Fun Is More Fun When Others Are Involved." *The Journal of Positive Psychology* 12, no. 6 (November 2, 2017): 547–57, https://doi.org/10.1080/17439760.2016.1221123.

7. Johnathan G. Fairman, "1st&2nd Laws of Motion," 1996, https://www.grc.nasa.gov/www/k-12/WindTunnel/Activities/first2nd_lawsf_motion.html.
8. Leslie L. Chang, Adam D. DeVore, Bradi B. Granger, Zubin J. Eapen, Dan Ariely, and Adrian F. Hernandez, "Leveraging Behavioral Economics to Improve Heart Failure Care and Outcomes." *Circulation* 136, no. 8 (August 22, 2017): 765–72, https://doi.org/10.1161/circulationaha.117.028380.
9. Angela Duckworth, "What Is Grit?" https://angeladuckworth.com/qa/#faq-125.
10. Audre Lorde, *Sister Outsider*. (Berkeley: Crossing Press, 1984), 44.
11. Jacquelyn Allen-Collinson, Lee Crust, and Christian Swann, "Embodiment in High-Altitude Mountaineering: Sensing and Working with the Weather." *Body & Society* 25, no. 1 (March 1, 2019): 90–115, https://doi.org/10.1177/1357034x18812947.
12. Robert C. Ginnett, "Crews as Groups: Their Formation and Their Leadership." In *Crew Resource Management* eds. Kanki, Barbara G., José Anca, and Thomas R Chidester. (London: Academic Press, 2019), 98.
13. John Beshears, Hae Soon Lee, Katherine L. Milkman, Robert Mislavsky, and Jessica Wisdom, "Creating Exercise Habits Using Incentives: The Trade-off Between Flexibility and Routinization." *Management Science* 67, no. 7 (July 1, 2021): 4139–71, https://doi.org/10.1287/mnsc.2020.3706.

Chapter 9

1. Alex Hagen, "Minnetonka Beach Woman Continues Alpine Skiing Success at 79." kare11.com, air date, January 23, 2020, https://www.kare11.com/article/news/minnetonka-beach-woman-continues-alpine-skiing-success-at-79/89-e255a6a8-3e14-46fc-856e-9f8ca70c18c8.
2. Catherine Yoshimoto and Ed Frauenheim, "The Best Companies to Work For Are Beating the Market." *Fortune*, February 27, 2018, https://fortune.com/2018/02/27/the-best-companies-to-work-for-are-beating-the-market/.

3. "We're Reshaping Retail in a Digital-First World." *T-Mobile Newsroom*, January, 2023, https://www.t-mobile.com/news/un-carrier/were-reshaping-retail-in-a-digital-first-world/.

4. David Lumb, "T-Mobile Continues Growth Streak With 1.3 Million New Customers." *CNET*, April 27, 2023, https://www.cnet.com/tech/mobile/t-mobile-continues-growth-streak-with-1-3-million-new-customers/.

5. Matthew Keys, "J.D. Power: T-Mobile Highest in Satisfaction among Postpaid Carriers." *The Desk*, July 2022, https://thedesk.net/2022/07/j-d-power-t-mobile-metro-customer-satisfaction/.

6. Quote Investigator, "How Can I Know What I Think Till I See What I Say? – Quote Investigator®." December 11, 2019, https://quoteinvestigator.com/2019/12/11/know-say/.

7. James Hlavenka and Pamela Meyer, "Deploying Agile as an Innovative Risk Management Framework in Pharma." *Food and Drug Law Institute* (FDLI), October, 2022, https://www.fdli.org/2022/09/deploying-agile-as-an-innovative-risk-management-framework-in-pharma/.

8. James Hlavenka and Pamela Meyer, "Deploying Agile," 2022.

Chapter 10

1. C. K. Prahalad and Gary Hamel, "The Core Competence of the Corporation." *Harvard Business Review*, May 1, 1990, https://hbr.org/1990/05/the-core-competence-of-the-corporation, digital reprint, 5.

2. Jade Salim, Ross Wadey, and Ceri Diss, "Examining Hardiness, Coping and Stress-Related Growth Following Sport Injury." *Journal of Applied Sport Psychology* 28, no. 2 (April 2, 2016): 154–69, https://doi.org/10.1080/10413200.2015.1086448.

3. Zenzi Huysmans and Damien Clement, "A Preliminary Exploration of the Application of Self-Compassion Within the Context of Sport Injury." *Journal of Sport & Exercise Psychology* 39, no. 1 (June 2, 2017): 56–66, https://doi.org/10.1123/jsep.2016-0144.

4. Cindy Kuzma and Carrie Jackson Cheadle, *Rebound: Train Your Mind to Bounce Back Stronger from Sports Injuries*. (London: Bloomsbury Publishing, 2019), 8.

5. The8thMotive, "Wide World of Sports Intro 1978." 2010, https://www.youtube.com/watch?v=P2AZH4FeGsc.

6. Pamela Meyer, *From Workplace to Playspace: Innovating, Learning and Changing Through Dynamic Engagement.* (New York: John Wiley & Sons, 2010).

7. Desiree Adaway, "We Are More Than Our Time, Productivity & Output." *The Adaway Group*, March 2023, https://adawaygroup.com/we-are-more-than-our-time-productivity-output/.

Chapter 11

1. Mary Brydon-Miller, Budd Hall, and Ted Jackson, *Voices of Change: Participatory Research in the United States and Canada.* (Westport, CT: Praeger, 1993).

2. Daniel K. Kahneman and Angus Deaton, "High Income Improves Evaluation of Life but Not Emotional Well-Being." *Proceedings of the National Academy of Sciences of the United States of America* 107, no. 38 (September 21, 2010): 16489–93, https://doi.org/10.1073/pnas.1011492107.

3. Richard M. Ryan and Edward L. Deci, "On Happiness and Human Potentials: A Review of Research on Hedonic and Eudaimonic Well-Being." *Annual Review of Psychology* 52, no. 1 (February 1, 2001): 141–66, https://doi.org/10.1146/annurev.psych.52.1.141.

4. Harvard Second Generation Study, "Harvard Second Generation Study," https://www.adultdevelopmentstudy.org/.

5. Robert Waldinger and Marc Schulz, *The Good Life: Lessons from the World's Longest Study on Happiness.* (New York: Random House, 2023).

6. National Academies of Sciences, Engineering, and Medicine, "Social Isolation and Loneliness in Older Adults." (Washington, DC: The National Academies Press, 2020), https://doi.org/10.17226/25663.

7. Robert Waldinger and Marc Schulz, *The Good Life: Lessons from the World's Longest Study on Happiness.* (New York: Random House, 2023), 97-102.

8. Benedict Nightingale, "Peter Brook, Celebrated Stage Director of Scale and Humanity, Dies at 97." *The New York Times*, July 5, 2022, https://www.nytimes.com/2022/07/03/obituaries/peter-brook-dead.html.

9. Arif Hamid, Jeffrey R. Pettibone, Omar S. Mabrouk, Vaughn L. Hetrick, Robert L. Schmidt, Caitlin M. Vander Weele, Robert T. Kennedy, Brandon J. Aragona, and Joshua D. Berke, "Mesolimbic Dopamine Signals the Value of Work." *Nature Neuroscience* 19, no. 1 (January 1, 2016): 117–26, https://doi.org/10.1038/nn.4173.

10. Tariro Mzezewa, "'Magic' on the Slopes: In Vail, 2,000 Black Skiers and Snowboarders Hit the Slopes." *The New York Times*, February 26, 2023, https://www.nytimes.com/2023/02/24/travel/african-american-skiers-snowboarders-vail.html.

11. Mzezewa, "'Magic' on the Slopes," 2023.

Chapter 12

1. Terrence E. Deal and Allan A. Kennedy, *Corporate Cultures: The Rites and Rituals of Corporate Life*. (New York: Perseus Books, 1982).

2. Gallup, "State of the Global Workplace 2022 Report." *Gallup, Inc*, 2022.

3. Randall Beck and Jim Harter, "Managers Account for 70% of Variance in Employee Engagement." *Gallup, Inc.*, March 28, 2023, https://news.gallup.com/businessjournal/182792/managers-account-variance-employee-engagement.aspx.

4. Gallup, "State of the Global Workplace 2022 Report." *Gallup, Inc.*, 2022.

5. Pamela Meyer, *The Agility Shift: Creating Agile and Effective Leaders, Teams, and Organizations*. (New York: Routledge, 2016).

MORE READING AND RESOURCES

Adler, Nancy. "The Arts & Leadership: Now That We Can Do Anything, What Will We Do?" Avital, M., Boland, R.J. and Cooperrider, D.L. (Ed.) *Designing Information and Organizations with a Positive Lens (Advances in Appreciative Inquiry, Vol. 2)*, Emerald Group Publishing Limited, Bingley, pp. 207-232. https://doi.org/10.1016/S1475-9152(07)00211-6

Alone, Unarmed and Unafraid, 2011. https://www.youtube.com/watch?v=IL5r5lve8k4.

Anchor, Shawn. *The Happiness Advantage: The Seven Principles of Positive Psychology That Fuel Success and Performance at Work*. New York: Currency, 2010.

Barrett, Frank. *Yes to the Mess: Surprising Leadership Lessons from Jazz*. Cambridge, MA: Harvard Business Review, 2012.

Brassey, Jacqueline and Nick van Dam "Don't Stress out: How to Build Long-Term Resilience," McKinsey & Company." December, 2018. https://www.mckinsey.com/business-functions/organization/our-insights/the-organization-blog/dont-stress-out-how-to-build-longterm-resilience.

Bryson, Ed. D. Naomi. *The Day Snow Turned Black*, AuthorHouse, 2008.

Chicago Metropolitan Ski Council—Racing, https://www.skicmsc.com/racing/racing_frontpage.htm

Christensen, Lisa, and Jake Gittleson, and Matt Smith. "The Career Advantages of Intentional Learners." McKinsey, August 7, 2020. https://www.mckinsey.com/featured-insights/future-of-work/the-most-fundamental-skill-intentional-learning-and-the-career-advantage.

Davis, Raymond, and Alan Schrader. *Leading for Growth: How Umpqua Bank Got Cool and Created a Culture of Greatness*. San Francisco: Jossey-Bass, 2007.

De Meuse, Kenneth P., Guangrong Dai, and George S. Hallenbeck. "Learning Agility: A Construct Whose Time Has Come." *Consulting Psychology Journal: Practice and Research*, 2010. https://doi.org/10.1037/a0019988.

Eichinger, R. W., and M. M. Lombardo. "Learning Agility as a Prime Indicator of Potential." *Human Resource Planning*, 2004.

Emmott, Mike. "Employee Engagement Is a Strategic Issue." *Strategic HR Review*, 0, no. 3, (April, 2010). https://doi.org/10.1108/shr.2010.37209cab.011

Eubank, Taylor. *Alone, Unarmed and Unafraid: Tales of Reconnaissance in Vietnam*. Ramtho Publishing, 2012.

Duckworth, Angela. "Find Your Grit in a Crisis." YouTube video, 35:18. May 4, 2021.

Gambill, Tony. "Why It Is Important For All Employees To Lead." *Forbes*. June, 2021. https://www.forbes.com/sites/tonygambill/2021/06/17/why-it-is-important-for-all-employees-to-lead/.

Handscomb, Christopher, Allan Jaenicke, Khushpreet Kaur, Belkis Vasquez-McCall, and Ahmad Zaidi. "How to Mess up Your Agile Transformation in Seven Easy (Mis)Steps." *McKinsey & Company*. April 6, 2018. https://www.mckinsey.com/capabilities/people-and-organizational-performance/our-insights/how-to-mess-up-your-agile-transformation-in-seven-easy-missteps?cid=other-eml-alt-mip-mck-oth-1804&hlkid=1b12a5f6df0a4cf3a47f9922ac09cecd&hctky=9800692&hdpid=9a62de33-9c77-4300-bbb9-bdcb3109ef73.

Hatch, Mary Jo. "The Dynamics of Organizational Culture." *Academy of Management Review* 18, no. 4 (October 1993): 657-693. https://doi.org/10.2307/258594.

Horton, Anisa Purbasari. "How Friends at Work Build Engaged and Inclusive Workplaces." February 14, 2022. https://www.td.org/atd-blog/how-friends-at-work-build-engaged-and-inclusive-workplaces.

Joly, Hubert. "Does Your Company's Culture Reinforce Its Strategy and Purpose?" *Harvard Business Review*, June 10, 2022. https://hbr.org/2022/06/does-your-companys-culture-reinforce-its-strategy-and-purpose.

Lincoln, Karen D, Donald A Lloyd, and Ann W Nguyen. "Social Relationships and Salivary Telomere Length Among Middle-Aged and Older African American and White Adults." *The Journals of Gerontology Series B: Psychologi-*

cal Sciences and Social Sciences 74, no. 6 (August 2019): 1053–61. https://doi.org/10.1093/geronb/gbx049.

Loveland Ski Club, https://www.lovelandskiclub.com/

Meyer, Pamela. "The One Question Agile Leaders and Learners Should Be Asking Now." Medium, April 23, 2020. https://medium.com/@pamelameyerphd/the-one-question-agile-leaders-and-learners-should-be-asking-now-d0374a151b30.

Mezirow, Jack, and & Associates. "Fostering Critical Reflection in Adulthood: A Guide to Transformative and Emancipatory Learning." San Francisco: Jossey-Bass, 1990.

Mortensen, Mark, and Amy C. Edmondson. "Rethink Your Employee Value Proposition." *Harvard Business Review*, January 1, 2023. https://hbr.org/2023/01/rethink-your-employee-value-proposition.

NASTAR (National Standards Race), https://nastar.com/.

National Brotherhood of Skiers (NBS), https://www.nbs.org/.

Peak Performance Ski Camp, https://peakperformancecamp.com/.

Rigby, D. K., Sarah Elk, and Steve Berez. "The Agile C-Suite." *Harvard Business Review*, 2020.

Rocky Mountain Masters, https://rmmskiracing.org/.

Rogers, Margaret. "A Better Way to Develop and Retain Top Talent." *Harvard Business Review*, January 20, 2020. https://hbr.org/2020/01/a-better-way-to-develop-and-retain-top-talent.

Ryan, R. M., and E. L. Deci. "On Happiness and Human Potentials: A Review of Research on Hedonic and Eudaimonic Well-Being." *Annual Review of Psychology* 52 (2001): 141–66. https://doi.org/10.1146/annurev.psych.52.1.141.

Schneider, Benjamin, William H. Macey, Karen M. Barbera, Valtera Corporation, and Nigel Martin. "Driving Customer Satisfaction and Financial Success through Employee Engagement." *Human Resource People and Strategy*, 2009.

Schneider, Marguerite. "A Stakeholder Model of Organizational Leadership." *Organization Science*, 2002.

"The Elusive Agile Enterprise: How The Right Leadership Mindset, Workforce and Culture Can Transform Your Organization." Report. *Forbes Insights*, 2018.

Styhre, Alexander. "The (Re)Embodied Organization: Four Perspectives on the Body in Organizations." *Human Resource Development International*, 2004. https://doi.org/10.1080/1367886032000150578.

Sull, Donald. "Competing through Organizational Agility." *McKinsey Quarterly*, 2010.

Szelwach, Celia. "Embodied leadership: Skills for the fourth industrial revolution." *Body Studies*. vol. 2, no. 6 (2020): 53-65.

Truss, Catherine, Amanda Shantz, Emma Soane, Kerstin Alfes, and Rick Delbridge. 2011. "Employee Engagement, Organisational Performance and Individual Well-Being: Exploring the Evidence, Developing the Theory." *The International Journal of Human Resource Management* 24 (14): 2657–69. https://doi.org/10.1080/09585192.2013.798921.

Varela, Francisco J., Evan Thompson, and Eleanor Rosch. "The Embodied Mind: Cognitive Science and Human Experience." Cambridge, MA: MIT Press, 1991.

Weick, Karl. "The Aesthetic of Imperfection in Orchestras and Organizations." Edited by Miguel Pina e Cunha, Joao Vieira da Cunha, and Ken N. Kamoche. *Organizational Improvisation*. New York: Routledge, 2002.

INDEX

A

acceptance 47, 105. *See also* Community

accountability 134

adaptation 68, 162–164, 165–166, 185–186

Adaway, Desiree 90–92, 183, 189–192, 199

affinity groups 109

agility. *See also* Embodied Agile Leaders, Leadership (EAL)
  Agility Shift Inventory™ 116
  Agile Transformations 150
  The Agility Shift (Meyer) 51, 89, 194, 232
  coaching questions 181–182
  commitment 150
  community 116
  competition 52, 89, 130–131
  defined 33
  happiness 215–218
  Meaningful Identity 176–180
  mindset 34–35, 89, 116, 175, 186–187
  shifts to 60–61, 175–176
  urgency of 52, 189

Alerus Financial 118, 121

Amabile, Theresa 129

amateur 3

ambassadors 226–229

ambiguity 16, 160

American Heart Association study 53

Andrews, Lilla Gidlow 127, 131, 171–175, 188–189, 210, 214

"anxious confidence" 66, 114. *See also* confidence

appearance 82–83, 89

athletes 67, 84, 135, 162

autonomy 46, 130, 131. *See also* control

awareness/attunement, assessments
  adaptability 41, 162
  Agility Shift Inventory™ 116
  coaching questions 55

embodiment 33, 62–65, 70, 160

of employees, team 229–231

risks 44, 55

strengths 184

B

Bandura, Albert 115

barriers. *See* challenges/obstacles

behaviors 53–54, 112, 116

belonging 47, 83, 105–107, 228. *See also* Community

biases 50–51, 54, 65, 158

Black, James (J.C.) 21

bodily sensations. *See* Embodied Agile Leaders, Leadership (EAL)

body language 120

Boyd, John "Forty-Second" 159

Brailsford, David 140

the brain, neurology. *See also* emotions

    belonging, relationships 47, 112, 119, 228

    biases 50, 54, 65, 158

    change of body state (COBS) 65

    fear 39, 45, 48–50, 53–54, 176

    feedback 140, 197

    gut instincts 32, 71, 230

    hormones 119, 215

    motivation 54, 130

    novelty 196

    self-preservation 33, 49

    telomeres 113

    uncertainty 46, 114

brand reputation 174

"brave space" 91, 92, 140. *See also* growth

Brook, Peter 214

Brumbaugh, Barb 136, 162

C

Cameron, Kim 119

Capy, Phil 210

certainty/uncertainty 16, 28, 46, 114, 160

challenges/obstacles. *See also* disruptions/changes

    anticipating, adapting 6, 14, 29, 33, 85–88, 184

    behavior changes 53–54

    challenge–support matrix 139–140

    change of body state (COBS) 65

    coaching questions 73–74

    discomfort 20, 40–41, 66–67

    identifying 55

    social-emotional 46, 157

    "what if" barriers 41, 48–49, 190

Cheadle, Carrie 192

Clark, Dave 80, 107–108

Clay, Art 217–218

coaching questions/reflections

agility, relevancy 181–182
commitment 165–166
community 122–123
competing, learning, growth 141–143
feedback 197–198
finding your why 36–37
happiness 219–220
Meaningful Identity 97–99
name, frame, claim your game 24
opportunities from obstacles 73–74
risk/reward assessments 55
strength, resiliency 202–203
value of 8, 197–198
co-creation 22, 108–109, 122–123, 231. *See also* collaboration
Cole, Dick 39, 129, 152, 155–156
collaboration 22, 160, 179. *See also* co-creation
comfort 22, 40–41, 66–67. *See also* challenges/obstacles
Commitment
  adapting, agility 150–152, 162–164
  coaching questions 165
  motivation, engagement 146–148, 148–149
  persevering 155–161
  prioritization 152–155, 231
  root word 103, 148
Community. *See also* relatedness, relationships

belonging 47, 83, 105–107, 228
coaching questions 122–123
commitment 148–149
competition 126–127
connectedness 112, 117, 130, 210–214
embodying 118–119, 217–218
fostering 105–109, 149, 230, 232–233
Google study 117
motivation 103
networking 116
participation 18, 107–109, 122–123, 230
"radical hospitality" 109–112
root word 103, 148
value of 105–107, 112, 116–117
compassion 192–193, 201
competence 46–47, 130, 185
Competition
  agility 130–131, 173
  coaching questions 141–143
  community 126–127
  embodying 136–137
  learning 134–136, 139–140, 230–231
  motivation 127–128, 214–215
  with others, self 128–129, 214–215
  root word 103, 128
complexity 16, 160
confidence 66, 114–115, 115, 120

connectedness 112, 117, 130, 210–214

control 49, 60, 134, 216. *See also* autonomy

cortisol 115

COVID-19 6, 29, 228

credibility 45–46

Creede, Cate 83

"crisis of meaning" 112

culture 89, 225–229

curiosity 111, 138, 214

D

daily stand-ups 151

Davis, Bryan 132, 134

Davis, Melissa 89

Deal, Terrence E. 225

Deci, Edward 129–130, 131, 133

discipline 146–147

disruptions/changes 17, 29, 34, 40, 200. *See also* challenges/obstacles

diversity 47, 106, 109–111, 117

dopamine 119, 215

Dotson, Tiffany 136–138

Duckworth, Angela 156

E

Eichinger, Robert W. 137

Embodied Agile Leaders, Leadership (EAL)

awareness, assessment 31–34, 41, 65–68, 160, 208–210

bodily sensations 63, 160

community, engagement 4–5, 51, 116–119, 236–237

culture 225–229

defined 16, 32–33

embodied reflection, understanding 59–64

perseverance, resiliency 157–161, 187–193

recognizing, recruiting, retaining 51, 232–237

strength 184–186

values 151–152, 225–226, 234–236

Embodied Reflection and Action Cycle Framework 69–73, 180, 229

emotions

belonging 47, 83, 105–107, 228

bias and 50, 54, 65, 158

compassion 192–193, 201

"crisis of meaning" 112

fear 39, 45–46, 48–50, 53–54, 176

gut checks 33, 71–72, 230

happiness, satisfaction 115, 118–121, 205–206, 210–214

negativity, positivity 50–51, 59, 65, 115, 119, 140, 187

pleasure 19, 133

social-emotional barriers, risks 45–48, 157
understanding 63, 160
well-being 81, 112, 130, 133, 200, 209
employees, employment
  assessing, evaluating 6, 29, 229–231
  company culture 106, 228–229
  engagement 29, 117, 147–148, 195, 228–229
  "the great resignation" 29
  recruiting 106, 147, 174
  relationality 118–121
  studies 6, 29, 86, 117, 228–229
  team productivity, success 118–121, 226
"endurance work" 158
energy, relational 119–121. *See also* relatedness, relationships
engagement
  "anxious confidence" 66, 114
  control 46, 231
  employee 29, 117, 147–148, 195, 228–229
  Meaningful Identity 84, 176
  motivation 133–134, 140, 152
  retaining EALs 51, 236–237
  studies 29, 86, 113, 117, 228
equity 47

F

failure 134. *See also* success

fairness 47–48
fear 39, 45–46, 48–50, 53–54, 176
feedback 59, 62, 140, 154, 174, 197–198. *See also* recognition
Ferstl, Max 102, 104
Field, Callie 117
Findley, Ben 217–218
flexibility 163, 185–186
Fortune 3
four Ps 18–23, 119, 130–131
Freier, Jon 174
FrieslandCampina Ingredients 60
From Workplace to Playspace (Meyer) 15

G

Gallup 228
the game. *See also* coaching questions/reflections
  feedback 197
  finding your why 36–37
  four Ps 18–23, 119, 130–131
  naming, framing, claiming 14, 21–23, 24–25, 79–81
  nature, energy of 18, 216
  participation 18
  staying in 28–35, 51–53, 173–174, 193–200
generosity 200–201

Gidlow, Lilla 126, 131, 171–175, 188–189, 210, 214

goals 54, 129–130

Google 117

Gregory, Dave 58–59

grit 156

growth 59–65, 139. *See also* learning

gut checks 33, 71–72, 230

H

Habitat for Humanity 90

habits 146, 163

Hamel, Gary 184

happiness
  assumptions vs. reality 212–213
  coaching questions 219–220
  competition and 214–215
  connection and 210–214
  embodying 208–210
  Harvard study 211–212
  hedonic, eudaimonic 209
  hormones 119, 215
  prioritizing 215–218

hardiness 192–193

Harvard Business Review 184

healthcare 93, 150

Hlavenka, James 92–95, 176–179

H&M 105–107, 147

hormones 119, 215

hospitality, radical 109–112

humility 57–59, 139–140

I

identity 91, 189–192, 200. *See also* Meaningful Identity

improvisation 15, 66, 206–207

inclusion. *See* Community

inertia 40, 57

innovation 19, 34, 214. *See also* disruptions/changes

intentionality 33, 62, 188–189, 196, 210

K

Keen, Amanda 3, 103–104

Kegan, Robert 81

Kennedy, Allan A. 225

K-Mart 52

Koenig, Melissa 49, 126

Kramer, Steven 129

Kuzma, Cindy 192

L

Landl, Karl 102, 104, 111–112

Lanier, Mike "Geronimo" 67–68, 145–146

Lanier Preston, Melissa 89

leadership 3, 33–34, 112–113, 222. *See also* Embodied Agile Leaders, Leadership (EAL)

learning
- agility 137, 174, 179, 196
- coaching questions 141–143
- continuous 63–64, 68, 136–137, 138–140, 214–215, 235–236
- growth opportunities 59, 139
- innovation 19, 214
- leading with 57–59, 62, 90–92, 137–138, 223
- motivation 127, 134–135, 215, 230–231
- play and 19, 86
- self-determination theory (SDT) 130–131
- *See also* challenges/obstacles

LeDoux, Joseph 65

Legere, John 88–90

Lombardo, Michael M. 137

Lorde, Audre 157

M

"marginal gains" 140

Marienau, Catherine 87–88, 104

Maxey, Miles 110

McCabe, Barb 114

McKay, Jim 193

McKinsey 6

Meaningful Identity
- agility, relevancy 88–90, 92–95, 176
- coaching questions 97–99
- defined 80–81, 86–89

"meaning-making" 81

naming, claiming, retaining 84, 108

"playspace" 86

supporting, validating 138, 213, 230

Mikulski, Chris 105–107, 111, 147, 175

mindset
- agile 34, 89, 116–119, 175–176, 186–187
- "anxious confidence" 66, 114
- shifts, adaptations 23, 31, 61, 68, 108, 162

Mirvis, Phillip 66

momentum 152

More, Abbie 4, 60–61, 156, 186–187

motivation
- commitment 149
- community 103
- defined 146
- extrinsic, intrinsic 53–54, 127–128, 133–134, 152, 215
- progress and 129–130, 140

N

National Brotherhood of Skiers (NBS) 110, 217–218

negativity 50–51, 65

networking 116. *See also* Community

The New York Times 218

Newton's law 152

Niemiec, Christopher 133

Norris, Dave "Chip" 118–119, 120, 132

O

observation 115, 159

obstacles. *See* challenges/obstacles

Ogino, Toshio 102

OODA (observe, orient, decide, act) loop 159–161

orientation 159

outcome, output 154–155, 163

oxytocin 119

P

Park, Peter 206–207

participation 18, 107–109, 122–123, 216–218, 230. *See also* Community

Paskowitz, Dorian "Doc" 84

passion 19, 90, 131, 156

performance 115, 127, 147, 154, 227

perseverance 155–161, 165–166

perspective 15, 48, 115. *See also* emotions

planning 60, 151

play 19, 86–87, 130–131

pleasure 19, 133

positivity 59, 115, 119, 140, 187

Prahalad, C.K. 184

preparation 45, 60, 158, 160, 194–195

presence 22–23, 34

prioritization 152–153, 163, 165–166, 199–200, 215–218, 231

progress 129, 135–136, 140, 163–164

purpose 19, 80, 90, 130, 147, 230

R

"radical hospitality" 109–112

recognition 129, 140, 149, 234–235

recovery 198–200

recruiting 147, 232–234

reflection 59–64, 68–72

relatedness, relationships 47, 112–119, 130, 210–214. *See also* Community

Relational Web 116, 213

relevancy 174–179, 181–182

renewal 198–200

resiliency 185–193, 202–203

resistance 40, 54

rest, restoration 198–200, 212

retrospectives 72, 151

risks 41–48, 55

Rock, David 45, 47

routines 146, 163

Routledge, Clay 112

Ryan, Richard 129–130, 131, 133

S

safety 49, 114–115

Sanford, Nevitt 139

scare tactics 53

SCARF (status, certainty, autonomy, relatedness, fairness) 45–48

Schulz, Marc 211–212

Sears 52

Seitz, Paul 210–211, 223–225, 227–228, 232

"self-efficacy" 115

self-awareness 33, 65. *See also* awareness/attunement, assessments

self-determination theory (SDT) 130–131

self-preservation 33, 49

Seppälä, Emma 119

setbacks 187–192

slowing down 67–68, 72, 188–189

Smith, Anna Deavere 109

Smith, Graham 158–159, 160–161

Society of Human Resource Management 29

Sprint 89

sprints 72, 151, 154

stand-ups 151

status 45–46

strength 151, 184–186, 200–201, 202–203

stress 114–115

success

characteristics, indicators 11, 116–117, 137–138

disruptions 17

dressing for 82–83, 89

failure 134

others' 226–229

suicide 112

support 139–140, 213

sustainability 151–152, 200

T

Taylor, Carol 19

telomeres 113

the game

staying in 28–35

T-Mobile 88, 117–118, 174

trust 161

U

UCB 93, 150, 178–179

Umqua Bank 194

uncertainty/certainty 16, 28, 46, 114, 160

US Department of Labor 86

V

validation 138, 149. *See also* recognition

value, values 151–152, 225–226, 234–236

VIU by HUB 132

VUCA (volatile, uncertain, complex, ambiguous) 16, 160

W

Waldinger, Robert 211–212

Weick, Karl 15

well-being 81, 112, 130, 133, 200, 209

WIIFM (What's In It For Me?) 51, 54, 231–232

WomenOver70—Aging Reimagined (podcast) 87

workforce. *See* employees, employment

Y

Yair, Gad 84

YouTube 217

Z

Zaki, Djemal 27, 30, 31

Zelitzky, Gail 87

Zimmerman, Mary 84

Made in the USA
Monee, IL
12 August 2023

40844996R00164